Burroughs and Friends

Lost Interviews

RE/Search #17

BURROUGHS AND FRIENDS:
Lost Interviews

ISBN 978-1889307-25-1

PUBLISHERS/EDITORS: V.Vale, Marian Wallace
ASSISTANT EDITOR: Andrew Bishop

RE/Search copy editors, staff & consultants:

Cecily Chen
Seth Robson
Robert Collison
Yoshi Yubai

Please check our website or contact us to find out about our full line of books and media.

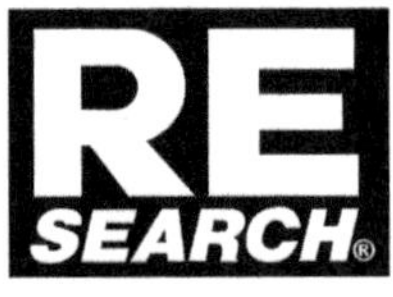

RE/Search Publications
20 Romolo Place #B
San Francisco, CA 94133
(415) 362-1465
info@researchpubs.com
www.researchpubs.com

TABLE OF CONTENTS

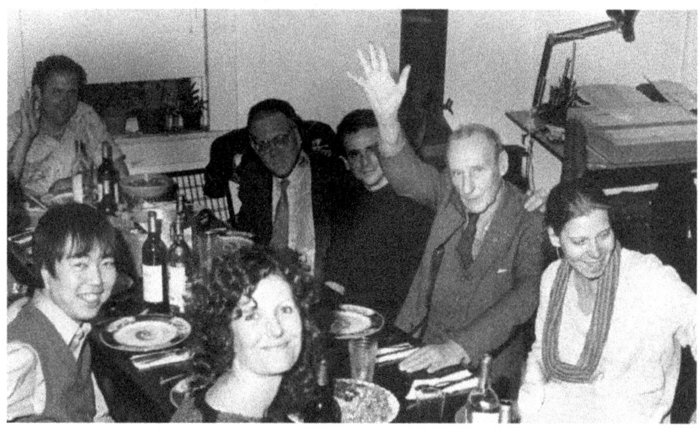

William S. Burroughs and friends at the RE/Search office, San Francisco

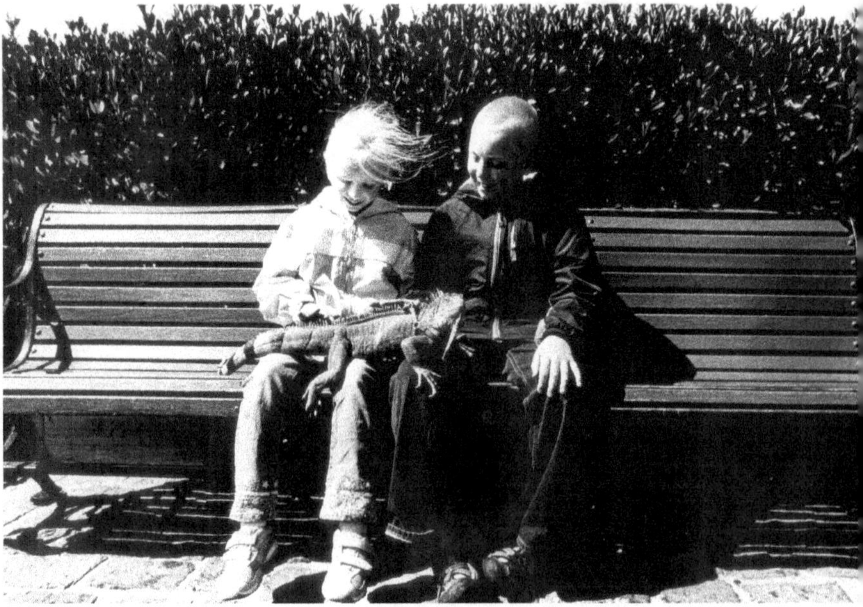

Photo: Yoshi Yubai

Introduction by V. Vale

It was quite a few years before I became a hardcore, committed William S. Burroughs "fanatic". I was lucky enough to live through the FSM (Free Speech Movement) at UC Berkeley (only recently I learned that Alice Waters was there at the same time) and "everyone" was talking about *Naked Lunch!* So I went and bought a Grove paperback edition but had a hard time "relating" to what I tried to read. Oddly enough, at the same time I was hearing about a book called *Naked Croquet* (a review talked about "people in the suburbs committing 'adultery' while experimenting with new types of social relations") so in my mind I must have conflated the two books!

I was genuinely puzzled when trying to comprehend Burroughs's "revolutionary" use of language and while his words could appear "dazzling" and shocking, I did not "fall in love" with this writing. Yes, anything to do with Dr Benway seemed very funny and instantly memorizable ("I can't be expected to work under these conditions!") but committed fandom remained years away.

Then, I saw an excerpt from a book of interviews with Burroughs by Daniel Odier; as I recall, it appeared in *Evergreen Review* magazine June 1969 before being published in *The Job.* Immediately I started memorizing quotes like "Belief is the enemy of knowledge"—yes! It seemed like everything "wrong" with the world had to do with "belief"—people blindly and unquestioningly "believing" in unsubstantiated words like "God" and "Jesus Christ" and "Allah" and "Jehovah"—and even worse, killing other humans using these words as an "excuse". It almost seemed like all the major problems with the world stemmed from LANGUAGE.

Burroughs railed against the use of the "either/or" syndrome—as George Bush later put it, "Either you're with us, or you support the terrorists!" (No, George, we don't support your trying to bomb the Middle East into the Stone Age, NOR do we support the "terrorists"—maybe some of us don't think America should be acting as the policeman to the rest of the world; what business do WE have interfering in another country's political system?).

Burroughs also seemed to be recommending the study of a non-linear, non-alphabetic language such as Egyptian hieroglyphs, or Mayan codices, or Chinese ideograms. Burroughs himself had studied Gardiner's *Egyptian Grammar* (he also recommended to me E.A. Wallis Budge's *Egyptian Language: Easy Lessons in Egyptian Hieroglyphics),* so I got myself a copy but frankly made very little headway toward the goal of mastering Egyptian hieroglyphs. I got *Her-Bak,* written by Isha Schwaller de Lubicz, and deluded myself by thinking I had made a little progress in this direction (the appendices in the back are very useful and repeatedly referential).

Given my seeming lack of ability to master Egyptian and Chinese, I thought the closest I could come toward non-linear thinking was embracing the Surrealist notion of "objective chance"—being open to chance whenever and wherever it shows itself. A bit later I learned about and embraced the notion of the "flaneur"—just taking random walks whenever and wherever you find yourself (this works particularly well in the old parts of Paris;

the arcades). San Francisco offered a number of obscure, interesting alleys and walkways on Telegraph-Russian-Nob Hill hillsides, even downtown (and probably neighborhoods all over the city).

Studying *The Job* gave me my goal in publishing: to focus on interviews. Why? Because when you publish a conventional manuscript, there's no challenging of ideas going on.

Burroughs was changing my life. I realized that the purpose of writing was to *change life.* I realized that people seemed to live their very lives by (to me) very "dodgy" words and phrases like "love" and "forever" and "eternal life" and "Jesus saves" and "trust" and—the list goes on and on. Why do people "believe" in all these words which have no verifiable "reality" or "substance" or "tangibility"?

Burroughs set me on a lifelong pursuit to *interrogate language*—a quest which never stops. It seems like *everybody* must set forth for themselves on this quest. Every single word "you" use in a way reflects and "defines" "you" (or your "identity"). I remember asking Burroughs if he had any "advice" and he attacked the generality of such a word, promptly ending with, "No, I don't have any so-called 'advice'!" Everything in life is specific. Everything in life is personal. There are no generalizations that can't be controverted or questioned.

That's our future: Question Until Death. (At least, life will probably be more interesting—maybe even more fun.) Certainly there will be more mystery in life. And mystery, as Duchamp told us, is the essential element of a work of art, a relationship, and probably, the rest of our life.

—V. Vale, January 2019

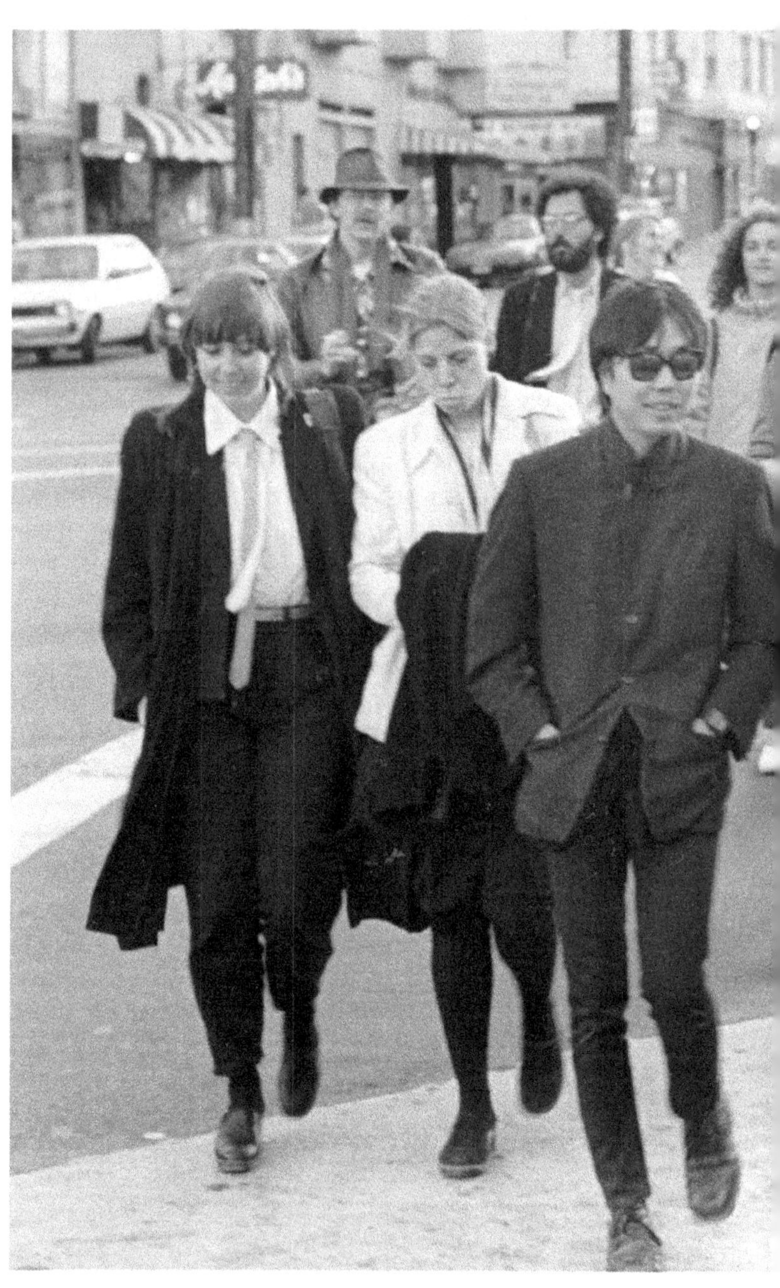

Photo: Chris Felver, from his photography book, Beat

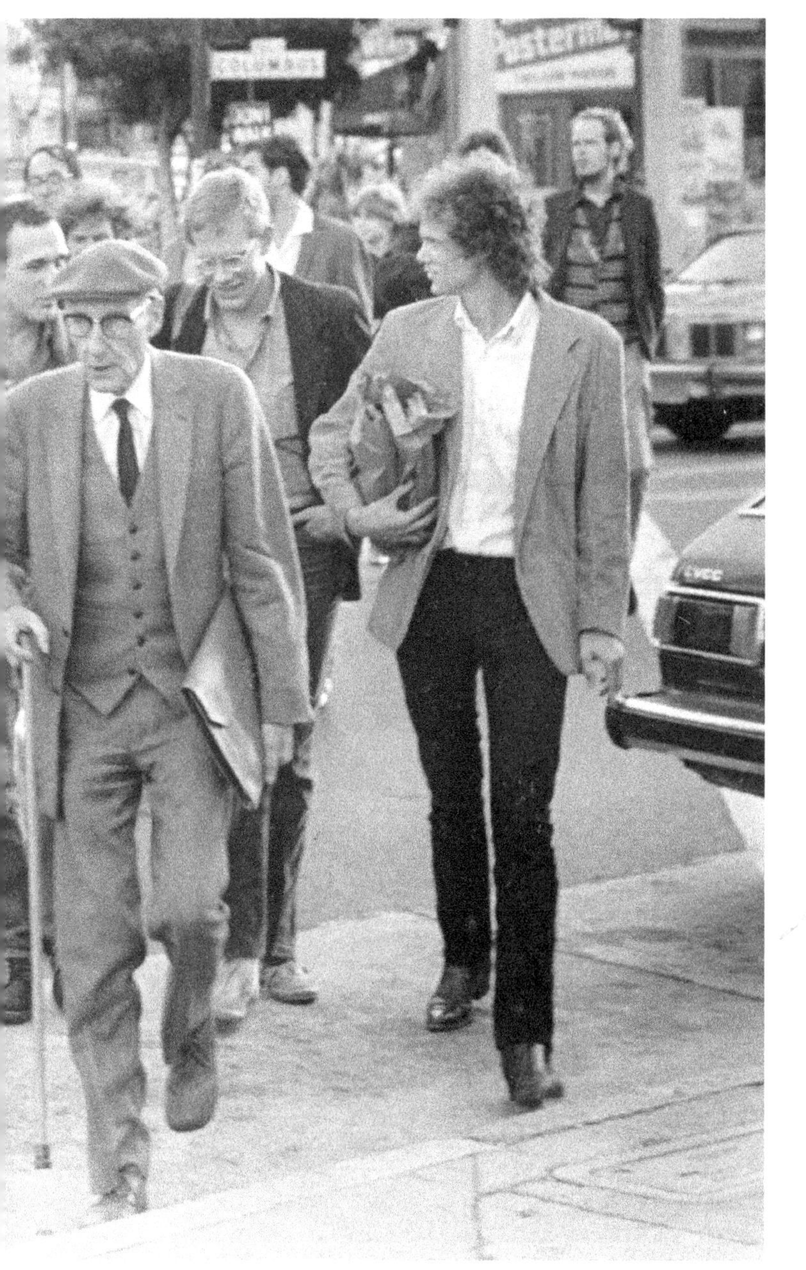

William S. Burroughs and friends on the way to City Lights, San Francisco

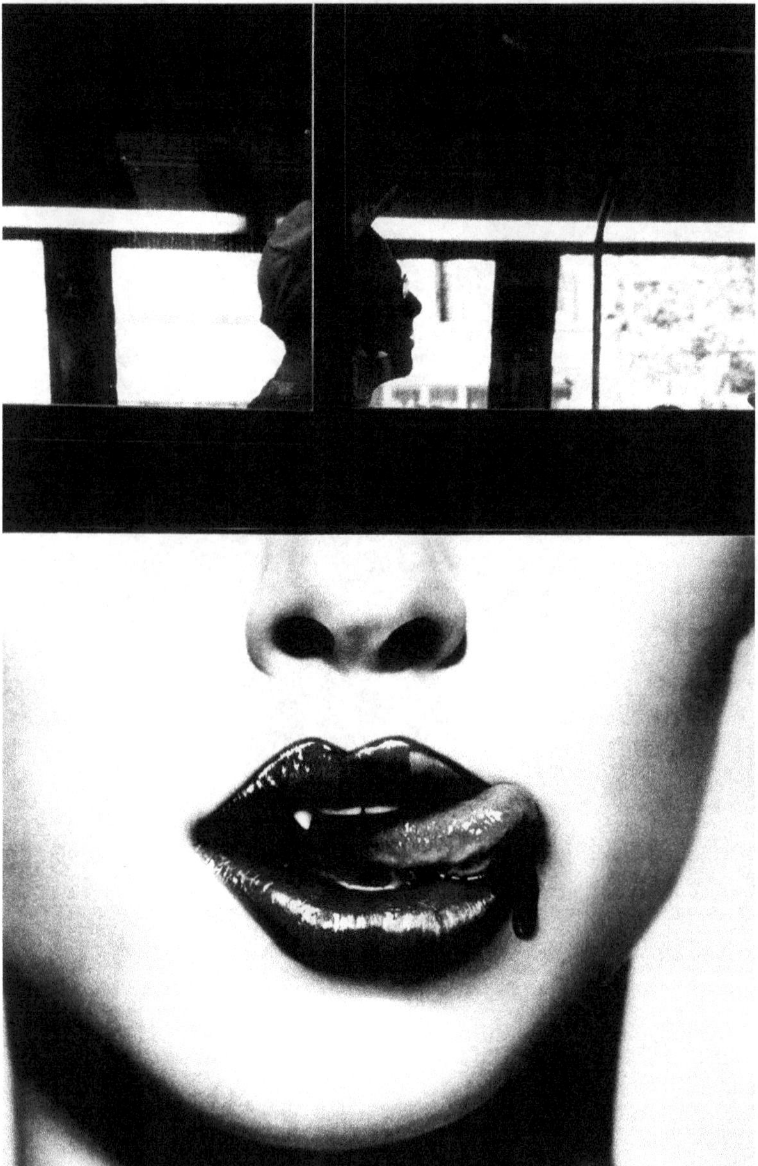

Photo: Yoshi Yubai

WILLIAM S. BURROUGHS: "Make America Great Again"

This previously unpublished interview with William S. Burroughs was taped at RE/Search headquarters in the early 1980s. Burroughs's novel The Place of Dead Roads *is being discussed.*

William S. Burroughs: I'll put out my cigarette—it's unprofessional, I think, to smoke during an interview.

RE/Search: In *The Place of Dead Roads*, it says, "Kim takes for granted that the only purpose of his life is space travel." How did that conclusion get reached?

Well, you don't *reach* these conclusions. A squirrel takes it for granted that he's arboreal and inclined to climb and live in trees. That's exactly the same situation: there are all sorts of *factors* that *condition* one. You don't just sit down and say, "I'm going to be a dinosaur, and I'm going to be big." Particularly if you've got an armored body sixty feet long and a brain the size of a walnut, as one of these models did—one of the dinosaurs. No, I mean their whole biological structure. And when I say, "I *decide*," I'm referring to some *tiny fraction* of my whole being and everything that I am in touch with. It's been compared very aptly with the conscious, linear ego: the tip of the iceberg that appears above the water. The decision has long been reached *way down* at the bottom of the iceberg.

It's self-evident, isn't it? It's self-evident to a squirrel. Or isn't it self-evident to a fish that he lives in a certain medium—a weightless medium? It is. It's self-evident to us that we are very much subject to gravity.

What is the origin of *Homo sapiens*?

Well, there's much debate on that. They keep pushing the humanoid discoveries back further and further; I think they're almost two million years now. **Perhaps we should just have an abortion and avoid the whole thing.** [laughs] I think two million is sort of the lunatic fringe, though. More conservatively, much less. Say, a little over a million.

What evolutionary changes are needed so humans can travel in space?

Oh, it would have to be very drastic, and of course, Darwin is pretty much *out* now. That is the idea that it takes countless eons to make an evolutionary change. So if man hasn't evolved, nor has any other species. It would seem to me that evolution is something that proceeds in quite sudden spurts, and then can be stable for millions of years. Now, this is the Punctuational—Punctuationist—theory of evolution. They've *got* to get a better name! The theory predicates that quite basic biologic changes can occur in two or three generations, in small isolated groups, where the equilibrium has been punctured. In other words, everything that they had taken for granted is suddenly gone, and then there are very *quick* changes. They did this with certain species of fish. [They] took a small number of them, and put them in a new environment, completely new, and there were all sorts of changes. Then when they brought in *enough* of these fish so they can set up a nation of, you know, like-minded fish, then the changes *stopped*. So if we're looking for biologic changes, we are committing biologic suicide with the increased uniformity of the human product. And there just isn't room for these little groups, it would seem.

To travel in space, we'd have to find something a great deal lighter; virtually weightless, in fact. While the astral body may have some weight, it has very little. It has some substance, so that's certainly a step in the right direction. But much more importantly, recent dream research clearly shows that dreams are a biologic necessity. As you keep people from dreaming by waking them up every time they have the rapid eye movements [REM] that indicate that dreaming is taking place, they soon show all the symptoms of sleeplessness. If the experiment was carried far enough, it would result in death.

Now, why is dreaming so vitally important? My feeling is that the dream is a link to our biologic and spiritual destiny *in* space, indicating a much lighter body that could, under certain circumstances, live without the three-dimensional.

The astral body is not without weight or consistency. It can be *felt*. It has some mass, but much less—so it's certainly a step in the right direction.

It is simply a projection of you—it's like your *Ka*, your double. Your spiritual double. It's exactly like the *Ka* in Egyptian mythology. They predicate seven souls. There's the *Ren*, the secret name, and that corresponds to my director, the one who gives the orders—the head man. Number two is *Sekem*, the technician. He's the one that presses the buttons and gets things *done*. He's always saying: these officers don't even know what buttons to push, or what happens when you push 'em. Three is *Khu*, the guardian angel, or bodyguard, etc. Now those three are eternal, that is they continue after the show—after the person is dead. See, the director films his life from beginning to end, and his secret name is the name of his film, what his life was all about. Well, for Nixon: Watergate. That's *his* film. Whatever.

So they go back then for another assignment. It's the four remaining that take their chances in the land of the dead. There's the *Ba*, the heart. That's all love affairs, *affaires de cœur*. Then there is the *Ka*. That's the most important you, because that's your double, and if *you* don't make it, he doesn't make it. So he's actually a reliable and honest guide. He has to be because his own interests are involved. And then there is the *Khaibit*, which is memory; and finally, *Sekhu*, the remains, the physical body. And there is one more, number eight: he who has these souls. Pharaohs had as many as fourteen. A pharaoh's dozen. They had two sets.

Is the *Ka* a magnetic field?

Yes, it's a magnetic field. It's what *animates* the human body. See, the human body—it's made of much the same material as this table, but it doesn't move of itself any more than this table does. Something *moves* it, and that is a magnetic field. Now, presumably a magnetic field, with enough knowledge, can be moved from one place to another… from one receptacle to another… certainly into another *physical* body, but perhaps even into a synthetic receptacle of some sort.

What can we do to use our dreams effectively?

What can we do to use our dreams effectively? Well, that will vary. The answer will vary: Who are you? What's your profession? Dreams are *vitally* important to a writer. I get fully a third of my material from dreams and write them down, and they sometimes are very vivid… a narrative that I only have to *transcribe*, like I've seen a very clear bit of film that goes into a work-in-progress. But for other people dreams have solved mathematical formulas. People have had mathematical or chemical formulas solved for them in dreams. I think they're useful, but it depends of course on what *use* the individual is making *of* them.

Are there any techniques to help us remember them?

Well, I guess you *could* keep a tape recorder. I always keep a pen and pencil [nearby]. But if the pen and pencil is across the room and you're sort of drowsy, very often you're just too lazy to go over there and write it down. But if you make a few notes, of course, that helps *immeasurably*. I can figure out—if I had forgotten a dream completely, and I see two words, it all comes back.

Had any good dreams lately?

No, they're not so common. I was thinking about—the last one I had was... I think about a month ago: a really good one. But they're varying. Some dreams seem to be completely uninteresting.

Kim's knowledge and mastery of magic and occult practices seem necessary to his survival. How could wannabe Johnsons learn more about and practice these?

Well, of course, there are a number of avenues. Finding a teacher—I have never had a teacher in that sense. A benefactor, as Don Juan calls it. But there are certainly many, many practices of meditation and martial arts or whatever that can help you.

I can think of *lots* of texts! Well, practically any sort of general knowledge text. I think some knowledge of the Egyptian system, which is unique with the seven-soul concept—*I* had already developed exactly the same methodology before I found out about this in [Norman] Mailer's book, *Ancient Evenings*. Because my actual knowledge of Egypt is very sketchy indeed—I fooled around a little with the hieroglyphs. Well, I think that's certainly one *key* there; any material would be good.

There is very little on Hassan-i Sabbah, the Old Man of the Mountain. There is a very good book by Betty Bouthoul, published by Gallimard in 1924, called *The Old Man of the Mountain* [actually, *Le Grande Maître des*

Assassins, 1936]. It was written in French, and I don't think it's ever been translated. Now that is one of the best. I don't know a great deal about tantric texts. I'd like to know more.

In *The Place of Dead Roads*, Kim sets out to organize the Johnson family. He soon finds himself in conflict with very deadly and very powerful forces—would you name any names?

Not physical names, no. Because it doesn't matter who is the actual man, because they are simply *representatives* of some power. Now the tendency of this power is seemingly

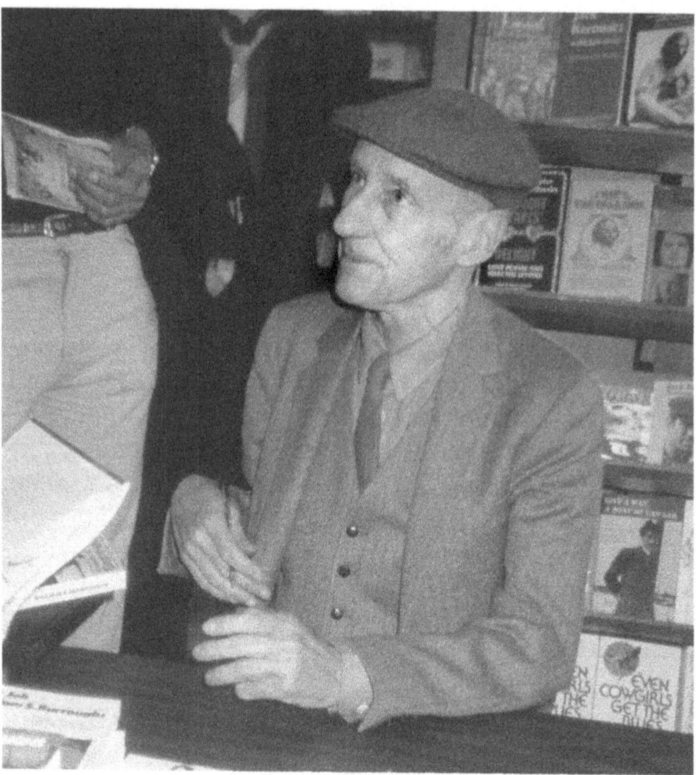

William S. Burroughs at City Lights, San Francisco

to keep human beings *right where they are* and to block them out of space. So they are always the authoritarian, the rigid, the dogmatic. All rigid dogmas from Catholicism to Communism have the same stultifying tendency and intent.

In the poem, *The Last Words of Hassan Sabbah*, you mention the Venusian cancer conspiracy, the Green Thing, the Short Dime Racket. Could you talk about these scams—

Well, they're all around us! In the first place. They are in a position to control our whole condition, our whole *input*. I mean we think that we are... We don't know how much is being *denied* us, because we don't find out about it. Since practically all basic discoveries have some military application, god knows how much really heavy *material* that could affect all sorts of very basic changes has been hidden away from us. But even on the surface, our whole circumstances, I mean... Take one conspiratorial route that no doubt exists. Conspiracies exist wherever there is a consensus of interest—whatever that interest may be. If it's big money—remember they control prices, interest rates, rents, all those things that are absolutely *basic* to the rest of us. And that, of course, is only the beginning. They have great control over *all* input.

I would say that you have to look *AROUND* you. I mean Hiroshima was a blatant step towards eliminating human inhabitants. Now I was invited to a 1984 conference which didn't come off, but... sociologists were saying that this is a world in which people are completely controlled by the people on top, and such societies could exist in a static form for thousands of years. Well, this is ridiculous because the first thing they would have to stop—if they wanted to exercise complete control, that is *mental* control—would be *dreams*, and all their loyal subjects would be dead in a few months! So this isn't a *forever* program, "a foot stamping on the human face forever," this is an *extermination* program, and can only be understood when you see it in those lights.

Now, if you want to get to the bottom of *any* situation, you always ask yourself: who profits? Well, clearly someone who had very different conditions of life from our conditions. And there seems to be some basic incompatibility there, although precisely what it is I wouldn't pretend to understand. I would just proceed on the face of what we *can* see.

You say the most powerful tool for manipulation is the "inner voice."

Well, I said it was *one* of the powerful modes of control, but it is not one that seems to be too easy to apply. We do know that when people hear voices, it seems to be an extraordinary experience. I'm quoting from Julian Jaynes, *The Beginning of Consciousness in the Breakdown of the Bicameral Mind*, who raises all these questions then backs away in horror from the answer. Yes, well, this man was walking along the seashore, and he heard this tremendous, vibrant voice telling him that he had to walk into the water and drown. And he described it as so loud that he couldn't understand how everyone didn't hear it on the whole beach—that it just went all *through* him. But most important: that he felt that he had to obey it. It was self-evident somehow that he had to obey it, which is very, very interesting indeed.

Now, we know that these voices, the origin of these voices, is the unused brain half. And indeed, we can produce voices in experimental subjects by electrical stimulation of the unused brain side to make people hear voices. Fix yourself on that. *Very important.*

Now, Jaynes—he said that the power of the priest-king derived from the fact that he could produce his voice in his subjects. They could actually *hear* the voice of the king in their heads. So it was like: this voice that's described that you *have* to obey was the *king's* voice, and it's with you all the time! *Imagine that:* you have the *complete* psychic control!

But he backs away from that, and he violently repudiates the idea of telepathy! I mean what is telepathy except producing your voice in someone else's mind. Telepathic experiments have usually been with pictures, which seem to work better. But this would be a form of *verbal telepathy:* very powerful. We don't understand exactly how it's done, but it would be easy to reproduce. If you had electrodes in the unused brain side of a subject, you could then by radio waves make him hear voices, and you could find out what the right combos were. You see, there are fear centers—there are different *centers* that you can touch. Now, this is quite within the range of present-day technology—to do it mechanically.

I'm sure that research along those lines is being conducted. Years ago, in Norway, they found they could produce voices in the mind of a subject by some electromagnetic field. It was sort of like a space helmet they put over someone's head. But how specific this was, how specific the voices were, I don't know. This solves the basic problem of intelligence, which is how the agent in the field can get orders and convey information without making a contact that reveals him to enemy intelligence. If they can do it like that, you see, that would obviate that whole necessity, so I'm sure research has been conducted both in Russia and in the United States. Well, this is very clearly stated in *Psychic Discoveries Behind the Iron Curtain* [by Sheila Ostrander and Lynn Schroeder]... the police use these telepathic methods. They always have.

You frequently mention Venus—why?

I am talking about a psychic locality which seems to be connected with the planet Venus, like these signs—

Aquarius, etc.—that has a very definite M.O., a very definite landscape as the way it looks, the way it acts, etc., that I describe at great length in my books, and very precisely. Well, after all, a writer is a mapmaker of psychic areas. So I am talking about an area, a psychic area, that I very extensively visited. If you ask whether it's real or not—well, it's as real as anything.

It's connected with the issue of why you might say, "Why anything? Why Saturn? Why Jupiter?" There is some equivalence in these astrological signs. I'm not into astrology at all. I mean, there's just an *equivalence* there that exists.

We have seen a terrific cultural revolution in the past forty years that was really unprecedented in the history of the world. It's much more of a general revolution than the liberal uprisings in 1848, and has made terrific changes. The whole thing about biologic alterations in space and all like that—it'll happen if species are left alone. You see, animals don't have this disadvantage: that the lions could say, "We can't permit the deer to mutate, they might get so fast we won't be able to catch them." So the deer is free to follow its biologic destiny, but we're not. We have all sorts of interference. So we direct our attention towards removing interference, but there's no *general* way of doing it; it's always in *specific* areas. We have seen, as I said, a terrific improvement and great gains! Good heavens—*the end of censorship!* All these were literally *bloody battles.*

Psychic weapons?

The psychic weapons are simply an extension of *you.* An astral extension of you—just a concentration on an objective. That's all. That's what I do in writing. And by clearly seeing an enemy and pinning it down on paper, you negate it! But pinning it down *wherever*. This is very old sort of psychic handbook stuff. Basic psychic self-defense, like how to recognize a psychic attack, and so

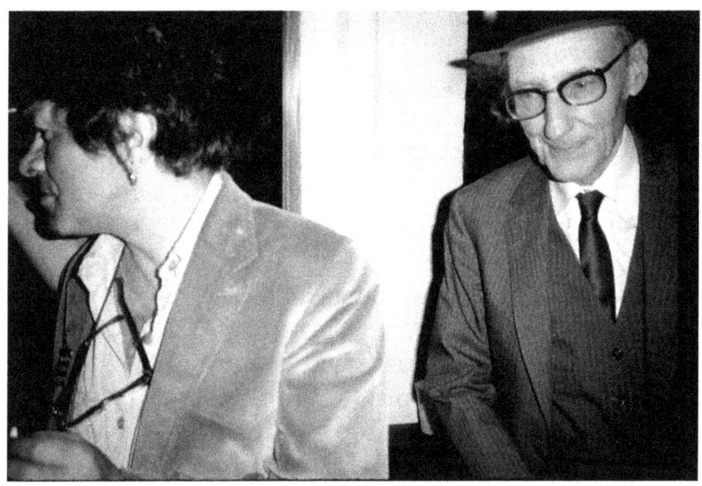

William S. Burroughs and Gregory Corso, San Francisco

on. Lots of people don't *know* how to recognize a psychic attack; they just don't know what's *wrong* with them... they think they've got the flu, or they're just feeling scared for no reason at all. Let alone take counter-measures.

What would be a tip-off?

The tip-off [laughs] would be the error. All this vague talk, you know... people suddenly have this bullshit *satori* where they see everything and everything is love. But when someone is trying to kill you, *you know it*, and you know it very precisely. Why, it's just like when an animal jumps on you!

In the book, William Seward Hall says that he can "unplot and unwrite" some people into random chaos. Can you elaborate on chaos?

Well, that's what writers are doing all the time—unwriting people into random chaos. That's the way they broke down censorship—by slowly writing the Bible Belt down into random chaos.

Would that be the same as scrambling someone?

No, not exactly. You're blocking them out of the significant areas, the control areas. Just as the Inquisition, you see, became less and less important: it was being progressively *blocked out* of any area where it could exert any control. They lost their police and their following…

Is that what you meant when you said you were working on a plan to pull down the sky?

Uh, no, not exactly. But this is the manifestation of Pan, God of Panic. Everything is a lie, including the sky! Yes, you could very literally pull down the sky under those circumstances. It's like everything is revealed as illusion, and people are quite *literally* rolling up the sky, bringing down the backdrops, carrying off the mountains!

How to survive?

Well, just by doing whatever you do, doing your job and doing it well. Alert passivity, all that.

What drugs would be most useful to take along on a combat mission?

It's dependent on the nature of the combat mission. Naturally, you need morphine, and cannabis is very useful to most people, myself included, for inducing a state of alertness and perception.

[Vale's cat enters the room and Burroughs begins to play with it] Yes! My little cat. Oh! What a beautiful beast. He's *unbelievably* beautiful! But I'm afraid he has a tendency to use his claws. You must get over that claw play. You must get over that claw play. God, what a beauty.

Immortality?

See, the Egyptian method was: you had yourself mummified. The physical body was very important, or was *essential*, to the continuation of the soul—the *Ka*—in the Western Lands.

You ask why this is, and you'll come up immediately with the answer that the whole thing was *vampiric*... that the mummies were vampires, and that they sucked their Western Lands from Fellahin blood! In fact, I have a partisan leader saying, "We're going to destroy all hell-fucking mummies, sucking heaven from Fellahin blood!"

So, for a vampire, you see, the physical body is vitally necessary—that's where he gets all his sustenance to keep him immortal. So it was obviously a vampire conspiracy, if you will. For this reason, you see, you can't have too many vampires, or they'll suck an area dry. Or they take a few centimeters here, and a few centimeters there—people hardly notice it. So it's got to be a good, tight club.

The method whereby the vampire gets his sustenance? No, they literally get out there and suck! Blood is always, of course, its equivalent—simply an equivalent of life energy. There's so much life energy in every being: their *Sekem* keeps them going. So the vampire comes and sucks some of this very literal life energy out to keep himself going.

What about the reduction to a virus?

Ah! Well, now you see the whole physical body contains the whole genetic code, as it were, for its vampiric *Ka* to operate. And you could reduce that cord—that *code* that spells out "Mr. Hart," "Mr. Rockefeller," just as the mummy of one of these people would spell him out, then you can do the same thing. You can take this virus, and insert it directly into a human receptacle, and then you can start sucking... good as any mummy.

Did Mr. Rockefeller have that done?

You know you're getting too *literal* there, but, *in a sense*, yes. He had the equivalent, the whole equivalent there, the whole *spirit* of vast wealth—that strange, withered creature—yes. He was just a *manifestation.*

"The Old Man found a way to bypass the mummy route." Could you explain that?

We don't know enough about it—Hassan-i Sabbah left no written words. I would suspect that it was sex between males—something very esoteric that he learned in Egypt. He probably found out how to merge his *Ka* with the *Ka* of his disciples, so they became, in a sense, one person, and that was the way that he controlled his agents from a distance. But that has to be inference. That's what I'm working on now, and I haven't gotten all that far. I just don't know. I'm trying to find out, in other words. I don't know yet.

Is sex a way to get beyond the duality?

Sex is a way of getting beyond a duality, yes! Because there's no necessity of maintaining the difference. See, the ego is maintained in a certain position by defensive mechanisms, and when those mechanisms leave, there's no *necessity* for defense. Then you'll have entrance to the Western Lands. That is the gate.

[Burroughs plays with the cat once again] Yes, my little beast… Yes…

What happens when we die?

What happens when we die? Well, different things for everyone. Your death is an organism—made, constructed—throughout your life. It has a different face for everyone. Death must always present the face of surprised recognition.

What happens when you die? Different things to different people. For some people it can come like a pistol shot; for others it comes slow... I would say that death presents a different face, or a different aspect, to every person. Usually, if they are at all distinguished people and worth death's trouble, then death will present the aspect of surprised recognition: the last person they ever expected to see, and yet somehow the most *perfectly* suitable. In fact, you might say, *deadly* suitable!

What happens in the physical death of an immortal?

Well, the physical death of the immortal, of course, is a contradiction in terms! He *wasn't* immortal! So, the same thing would happen to him as happens to anybody else. You see, in many mythologies, there are all sorts of creatures who are only *semi*-immortal. Vampires, for example, or mummies, are semi-immortals because someone comes and destroys the mummy or finds the physical body of the vampire—see, they're exactly the same—and destroys that body and impales it, or burns it, or otherwise destroys it, then the vampire is completely fucked. So there are semi-immortals, and there are lots of beings like that—that is, spiritual beings—which are not as solid as we are, but which certainly can be killed.

Can you describe the astral plane where these immortals existed as vampires?

Well, that would be very varied, according to their dispositions, etc. But I think I have touched on it frequently in my work. Some seem to be in a very cool, very cool blue area. I think there are various... Quite a variety of condominiums.

Could you describe your experiments in the progress you've made towards immortality?

It isn't a matter of experiment. As Don Juan says: your death is *always* with you, and the trick is to confront it at all times. Insofar as you confront your death, you are immortal, which is why an act of courage always gives a terrific feeling of exhilaration, like a successfully completed parachute jump or anything like that. It's also a very *dangerous* state.

What about astral and time travel?

Well, you see, astral and time travel are things that take place twenty-four hours a day. All you have to do is to put yourself back to where you were an hour ago. Well, I think astral and time travel takes place all the time when you put yourself back where you were an hour ago, in a sense you *are* "back there"… a question of degree. And all dreams certainly can be interpreted as astral and time travel. And, of course, one of the most frequent—or, very frequent—features in my work, for example, both *The Place of Dead Roads* and *Cities of the Red Night*, are *predicated* on time travel. I wouldn't say exclusively concerned, but certainly predicated on time travel.

You write, "In the beginning of time was a deed so foul that we've been fleeing from it ever since."

That quotation is from *The Hounds of Tindalos* [by Frank Belknap Long]. A very good story. Nobody has been able to come up with a good answer. He just said: a deed so foul we've been fleeing from it ever since. Well, it *must*, inferentially, have the *shape* of our flight. You get a lot of people—they're all fleeing from the same thing for millions of years—that thing is going to show itself in the configuration of the flight, insofar as it will show itself *at all.*

As for the deed, nobody knows what this deed is. Of course, you can't sell Hollywood on that: you've got a monster picture, but you don't produce the monster. But frankly, no one has ever *found* the monster, or even a *partially* satisfactory explanation for the origins of human speech—or what speech IS, for that matter.

"The human voice as the ultimate weapon": could you elaborate?

Well, if we *knew* these things, we could reduce whole populations to silence. Just black out their whole communication system... That would be an ultimate weapon: no one can give an order!

Could you summarize as many fundamental defects or lies in Western language as possible, e.g. talking about the "either/or," the "to be," "the"—?

Oh: *errors in Western language...* [Alfred] Korzybski has written an excellent book on this subject called *Science and Sanity* and I think there are condensations of this book available from the Non-Aristotelian Society.

Well, he pointed out that "either/or" is one of the basic flaws in all Western thinking, like "either intellect *or* emotion" instead of "both... and..." Because every action is both intellectual *and* emotional. For example, your cat wakes up and he feels hungry—that's an emotion, an instinct, but then his *front brain* goes to work to show him *where food has been, there food will be.* This is still the basic guiding principle of Hollywood: what *has* made money *will* make money. But as soon as that happens, the cat's front brain is going into operation, taking him to where the food will be—same way with people. So, trying to chop the human body into intellect and emotion... I mean it doesn't at all correspond to what we know of the human organism and the universe.

So there's a basic flaw. Another is the definite article, as though it was a *permanent: The* God, *the* way, instead of *a* God, *a* way. And another is the *is of identity*, as though this were a permanent status. "He *is* my servant." Now, the Egyptian's glyph: "He *as* my servant." At this moment, he is *acting as* my servant. "The 'is' of identity," Korzybski calls it.

Well, next are general words like "communism" and "fascism" and "democracy" and "civilization"—about which everyone has practically as many definitions as there are people that *use* them. So Korzybski says that instead of definitions, let's have *descriptions*. Instead of talking about communism, let's talk about the actual political configuration as closely as possible.

I think those are the main ones… Oh, and generalities. Yes, this is a very important one, particularly for all journalists: *Who did what, where, and when?* "It is generally *assumed* that…" By *whom* is it generally assumed? "The consensus of medical opinion." Well, Mr Anslinger was talking about "the consensus of medical opinion is that the use of cannabis invariably results in insanity." And his consensus of medical authority came down to one Indian physician of very *dubious* qualifications, who considered the use of marijuana a reason for incarceration in the mental hospital—and that, of course, *proves* the thesis. But usually when anyone says, "It is generally…" or, "All civilized men will agree that…" someone's gonna dump some *outrageous* piece of nonsense in your lap.

Does language shape neurological patterns?

Well, yes! We don't know to what extent—or, if people didn't talk, what they'd even *look* like!

You talk about time as a resource. Time runs out.

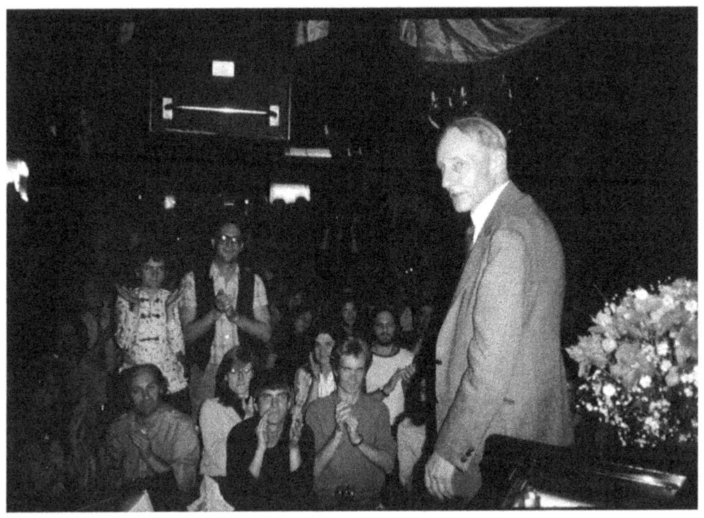

William S. Burroughs at Keystone Korner, San Francisco

The most fundamental problem facing any culture is the conservation and disbursement of time. How do the controlling forces manipulate this resource to our disadvantage?

Well, there are many answers to *that.* It depends entirely on what civilization you are talking about. Of course, the English sort of "muddling through things" *seems* very efficient. But when you see the change—that time is measured in terms of change, human change... So something that tends to *block* change, while it may *seem* very time-consuming, is actually a time-*conserving* device. "Very ill-advised at the present time", and then "don't go too far in any direction"—is another basic English dictum.

So time, the disbursement of time is abused in many ways by those at the top to the detriments of those below them. The Mayan Priest had a rather complete control of time—there was a continual round of *festivals.* And, of course, well: Catholic ritual and so on, and saint days—

those are time-controlling, time-occupying devices.

So change would lead to the end of a particular civilization? And those in charge don't want change, so in that way, they stop time?

No. You see, there's always a paradox. While they'll tend to keep things as they are, they're intelligent enough to know that they can't do this, that this would even be a very dangerous thing to do: to try to hold something together that just can't hold together anymore. It's like trying to control inflation. But they want to *minimize it*—that's all. It's a very sort of hit-and-miss, piece-out-the-odds, short-sighted policy.

Does time relate to immortality, in the sense that being above time is to be immortal in a sense?

Yes, exactly. Yes, I'm talking about *the transition from time into space.* It's as drastic as the transition from water into land.

Page 217 in *The Place of Dead Roads*, "To put it country simple: the Christian God exists." That's an astounding statement! How did you come to that conclusion?

I don't think it's astounding *at all!* Everything I've been talking about is what we see, the input from the Christian God. Well, whether you call it the Christian God or not, it is a very powerful force, which has molded practically the whole of Western civilization for two thousand years. I think one reason for the general *appeal* of Christianity is that it appeals to the lowest common denominator. "You're all going to get this immortality if you just *BELIEVE.*" Well, now, biologically speaking we know that it may come down to one in a billion is

Photo: Yoshi Yubai

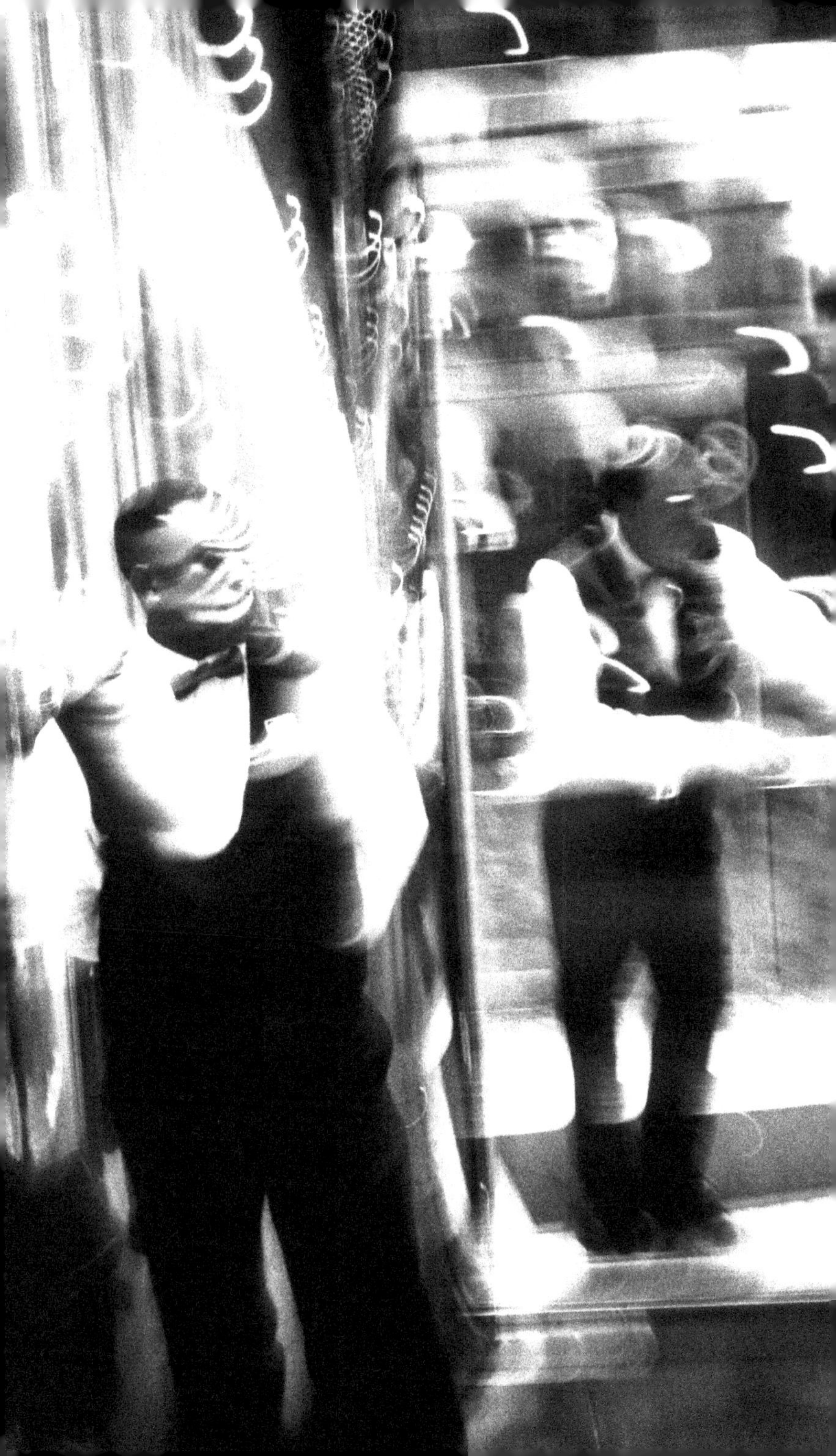

going to make it—and these are good odds, biologically speaking. But they're not *popular* odds. People don't want to hear about one-in-a-billion odds. No, they're *all* going to get it, just if they sit there and believe, and whine out a sniveling prayer.

There's the belief that the Christian God will control history, and there'll be some sort of Armageddon which He will win. Well, I see no reason to believe that. That's what they *want* people to believe, but I don't see much substantiation.

Naturally, if this is their idea, they're working to realize it. But of course, there's this terrific split: the people at the *top* don't believe all this rubbish. And there's the difference between what the people at the top believe and what they give out to the masses, I imagine…

With respect to the pre-recorded human films, how does one rewrite one's destiny?

Well, by rewriting it. Cut-ups are one way: "It is written" and you chop what is written! Of course, if you could get to the *pre*-recordings, then you'd be chopping the actual fabric of reality. But the one thing not pre-recorded in a pre-recorded universe are the pre-recordings *themselves*. Now there are ways in which you can tamper with that.

Well, *Ren*, your secret name, the director from the front office—you get your own director in, which I did in *The Place of Dead Roads*. That is, Hall is another director. And the other director under the control of, or acting in concert with Bickford and Hart—there, then we have two directors balanced against each other in a contest. Whereas according to the pre-recorded universe, there should only be one; that there should be another is intolerable, as it could destroy the whole pre-recorded universe. One hole and the whole thing comes toppling down because it *is* pre-recorded. (It isn't doing anything new, in other words.)

Can you name any techniques to bring that about?

Well, I was just talking about getting another director! That's for every man to decide. I do that—that's what I'm doing in *The Place of Dead Roads,* is introducing another director. And, of course, cut-ups—in a sense, they're cutting what is written. That is, cutting sections of time and moving them around… cutting the time and image minds of a pre-recorded universe.

You talk a lot about being able to do cut-ups and take pictures and make tape recordings by a place, and go back and play them back and take more pictures, and this will bring pretty serious problems to where you do this. How does this work?

No idea. Just know that it does. And it's *used,* very extensively.

What Gods, if any, would aid us in future survival?

Well, I've talked a lot about that in *The Place of Dead Roads*. Hassan-i Sabbah, although he isn't exactly "Gods." Hassan-i Sabbah, Pan—God of Panic. Huwawa, Master of the Future, Master of Abominations. There are many. But *all* the old gods! The Gods of the Mayans, the Gods of the Indians; the American Indians. The East Indians. A whole pantheon.

How would we invoke these Gods?

In different ways. Good heavens, there are very detailed, and very arbitrary descriptions in all occult books that suggest how this is done and all this stuff you have to go through. I think myself that it's time for them to come out of the circle and into the street with all this. I said that in an introduction to the *Necronomicon.* I just don't follow all this absolutely arbitrary ritual of certain incenses and herbs and words and so on.

Are there occult secrets that are not being told?

None of them are being told, hardly. Well, you read through a lot of these occult books, you may find a little hint here and there. But by and large, no.

If you knew any secrets, would you tell them?

I tell all I know in my books!

How does one know what occult books are disinformation, so to speak, and which ones are the real thing?

You *don't*—in any other subject, either. Well, yes, you have a consensus of opinion. I mean, well, we all know that Proust books are worth reading, and certain scientific theories are completely discredited, and so on. You have just a common sort of knowledge. There are a few good books. David Conway wrote a very good book, *Magic: An Occult Primer*—one of the better books. Crowley, I find awfully long-winded. He may have been a good magician, but he certainly isn't a good writer! So there isn't so much of it—it seems to go nowhere.

Well, the seven souls of the Egyptians I found very interesting. Little bits of information like that, gleaned here and there.

I assume it's dangerous to experiment with that—

Well, it's dangerous if you get *close*. Very few people do get close at all.

How did the Judeo-Christian Bible come to have

such enormous power and influence?

Well, partly because it appeals to the common denominator, but the same could be said of the Koran, which has numerically almost as much extent, I think. It certainly has about as much circulation, when you consider how many Muslims there are. I don't know how it stacks up. I don't think any other books have that same absolute appeal to the common denominator: that all you have to do is to obey certain rites—even giving lip service—and you'll be *all right*… you will be immortal.

How can one tell if a person is an informer or an infiltrator?

Well, there's a very easy test: a polygraph will do it in five minutes. I spent a lot of time with them, and I state that people can't beat them. They have all sorts of systems that they think work, but if the person giving the test knows what he's doing, it's very hard to get around it indeed.

And now, of course, they can do the same thing with just voice recordings, and I should imagine they are very, *very* reliable. See, the C.I.A. considers it grounds for dismissal, so it means they must take it very seriously, indeed. They've trained somebody, and then they call him a "flutter." They have to report him for a flutter if there is any doubt, and I think they have periodic flutters in unpredictable times. They'll have one, and then everybody thinks that's over for another year, and then they'll pull another three days later—and all that sort of thing.

It seems that wannabe Johnsons would do well to pattern their actions somewhat after the C.I.A.—

Yes, well, there are certain techniques of any organization that carry over to any organization. There are certain basic laws of guerrilla operations that are the same wherever you operate, or on whatever level.

Do you think the current administration might provoke an incident to justify the imposition of martial law?

Whether the present administration would ever provoke an incident to give them a pretext for martial law, I doubt it very much—it's a very *dangerous* thing for them to do, and why should they do it? Because once you've made that step, then you have to make other steps, and they're all very dangerous.

You see, we have never had that gap between the military and the civilian administration, which occurs in practically all Latin American countries, where any general can suddenly grab the presidency. But, once you start declaring martial law, you're going in that direction, and this is a very, very dangerous thing for the civilian administration to do—to invoke martial law. And then what are you going to do with them? They soon realize that *they* have the force.

So actually the civilian administration would be giving over their power to the military if they invoked martial law?

Exactly, yeah. It's an old, old problem. Yes.

It's been reported that the LAPD has acquired Uzis with silencers. Can you imagine any legitimate reason for police to have Uzis with silencers?

Yes, but only in SWAT operations. I think that's probably, you'll find, what they're used for. They're not for general use at all. And there [in SWAT operations] they do have a definite use.

Meaning to pick somebody off without others hearing the shot?

All that. They've got somebody, more than one person, holed up in a house, and suppose they break in the back door and shoot one of them. It would be very advantageous to have the shot silenced so the people in front wouldn't know that someone had broken in. But I think that'll be the only use.

What specific steps do you think Reagan will take as he's hinted toward returning this country to "old-fashioned morality"?

Reagan is talking about getting back to the old versions, but that's just this old politician horseshit. They've been saying it for a hundred years: "Back to the virtues that made America great and can **make America great again**!" It's not to be taken seriously, of course. Biologically speaking, the only direction you *can't* go, is back! It's impossible. It's a law.

How would you assess Reagan's impact on the country?

I don't think it's been all that heavy, really. There is no doubt that he has cut public expenses to the very real detriment of certain of the people living on welfare and small-fixed pensions—no doubt about that. But I don't think it's been very *heavy*. He has come out definitely with his Central American policy, which I think is *unwise* and could get us into some real problems of involvement.

Do you think that AIDS was introduced by design?

It's hard to say, but it certainly acts as if it *could* have been. It's blocking evolutionary avenues.

Any new, interesting developments in police-state surveillance and control technology?

Oh, new developments in police-state surveillance and control technology. Well, in a sense, of course, it's already gone so far, and you can't see how it can get much further. The electronic methods of control, you see. With electrodes implanted in the skull, they can control thought, feeling, and apparent sensory impression. They can make the thought of rebellion physiologically impossible.

But what they have to do is to strike a balance. If you go too far towards control, you're going to kill your subject. I don't think any organism could *survive* being completely controlled. And if you don't use it, you lose it! So if they go too far, they're going to kill all their subjects. So they have to, sort of, you know, give a little and take a little. *Jockey around.*

Do you like traveling?

Well, of course, yes! Traveling is very special, and while you enjoy it and it's very rewarding to meet people who read my work—that's why they come to the readings, as a rule—but it's something that you can only do for a brief period of time. I recently had a Scandinavian tour. Well, it started in America. I made about ten or fifteen stops over the period of about five weeks, and while it was very enjoyable and interesting, nonetheless I was glad to get back. Because I can't *work* at all on these trips, so I had to get back to what I'm doing. I had to get back to work.

Did you do anything special to stay vigorous?

Well, I walk. Get out and shoot and fish, sometimes. And I like to get out in the country for an afternoon every chance I get, yes.

Some longevity serums are based exactly on that

principle of *stimulating the resistance;* anti-human injections, they called them. That was the Bogomolets serum. I see no evidence that it actually worked, though.

You said in *Naked Lunch* that America was old and evil, even before the Indians got here. The evil was there, waiting for them. Can you elaborate on that?

Not particularly, but I know that areas *are* evil. You can get even areas in a city that are bad. I remember this one block on Prince Street, between Mulberry and what's the one over? Mulberry and then Chinatown, going that way. I'll remember it in a minute. [Mott Street?] *Always* something nasty going on there every time I passed! And you can *spot* these areas in a city—nasty areas. So the same could apply to whole localities. Even for thousands of years, there are bad areas, *bad land*—it's just a *bad place*, like a bad house, or a jinxed ship.

Are there secret societies that have gone on for thousands of years?

Well, obviously! We know of them. The Masons have gone on for quite a long time. And some of the upper reaches of Catholicism, I think, amounts to a secret society: the real "elite." There are certainly so-called backward areas, all these tribal societies. Yes, certainly there are. Well, if they were really "secret," we wouldn't even know about them! Right?

Well, what are they up to?

Different things! All different things according to their orientation. That is, the Masons are very definitely into white supremacy and very tight oligarchical control. That's what they're about. Other groups are into very different things.

As I say, there are many of these groups, and they all have leaders and local leaders. Some of them are fairly large. Well, look at the—what do you call them… the Sikhs. They have a lot of money, and a lot of places around America, the Sikhs and the Moonies. Those are small ones but oh yeah, there are lots of these societies with initiations, and you get up, up and up in the thing. Something called a thirty-three-degree Mason, I believe. And above those are Blue Masons.

What are people like Sun Myung Moon and Rajneesh trying for?

I don't really know. Well, they're trying for *advantage* in the widest sense. Oh yes, they're probably very much consistent with [L. Ron] Hubbard of Scientology—that is his principal *concern,* is immortality—he's always talking about it.

You said that you didn't want to "give out" Hubbard's couplets because he's claiming some "right" to them. Have you ever rethought that? Of exposing—

Well, I don't think there is anything much to "expose" there, really.

Well, you said that there is a set of three hundred contradictory—

Oh yes, there are lots of little couplets and problems and "processes," as he called them, to have certain success. Like: what is the problem, what solutions do you have to that problem—you finally realize that all your solutions have created *more* problems. Sound enough, some of it.

[Tape cuts out]

—the dictionary. In other words, they're using a lot of long words. You see, when someone gets to a long word, and he doesn't understand it, it gives him, for one thing, a feeling of inferiority, because he feels that he *should* understand it. And if he gets about three or four of those, he doesn't want to *know* about whatever is in front of him. So that's a very definite technique, enunciated by Hubbard for producing in the mind of the reader an unfavorable impression of whatever he's talking about. Very precise illustration, I think.

You're traveling now—

I travel quite a bit, so if I do give a reading, I get to know the people who are interested in my work—that is, readers and fans and so on. That is a *very* rewarding aspect of giving these readings: I meet people who have actually read the books! And a lot of writers don't.

A reading or a book signing—they're the same.

What do you think of the Howard Brookner film about you?

I think it's very competent and very good.

Are humans violent by nature?

Well, *potentially*, yes. We *all* are if we intend to stay alive—this is a war universe. It's what the universe is all about, is war.

You've talked about your life being "a fight of resistance against an ugly spirit"—

Well, yes. Well, that is, I think, true of every man. That everyone has an antagonist... something parasitic,

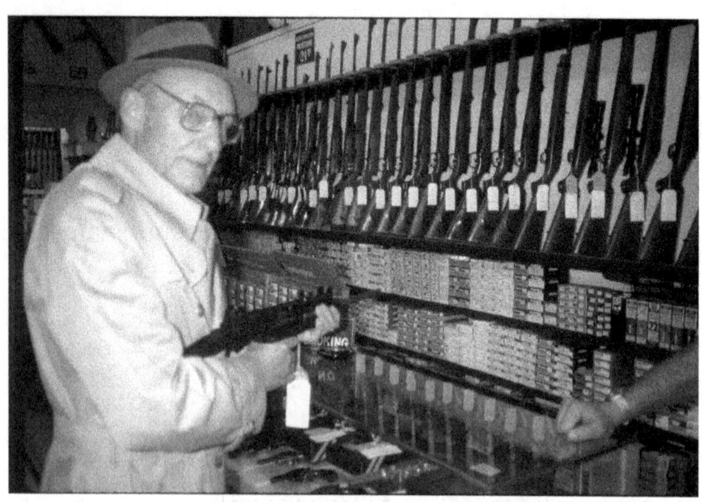

William S. Burroughs at the San Francisco Gun Exchange

presumably. It's an age-old combat.

Lucien Carr accused you of having "Boy Scout morals"—

Well, I don't know what he *means* by "Boy Scout morals," but I certainly believed in some so-called "old-fashioned virtues" like courage, loyalty, honesty. I think a man's word should be good. I think that people who refuse to help—like, forty people stood around and watched while a discharged mental patient stabbed someone to death in Central Park. And they did absolutely nothing! That's terrible! I would have intervened immediately! I always carry *some* weapon. I'd have done whatever I could *do*.

So you carry a spring-loaded Cobra [baton]?

I always carry that.

Do you ever use it?

Never had to, no. Knowing that it's there is probably why I've never had to use it.

When you were sitting in a hotel room in Tangiers looking at your toe under the influence of whatever substance you were on—

That's what's known as an "oil burner" habit! I didn't think much further than the next fix, usually.

To what do you attribute your longevity?

Well, just being alive! What I had was a *drug habit.* It isn't injurious to your health. To characterize it as disease—it's not true! George Crabbe, an English poet, lived to be 90 [actually 77], and he was addicted to opium for 50 years. An addict takes a certain dosage every day. You don't *use* needles to take it orally. He lived about as long as everyone else—maybe longer. It doesn't compare to alcohol—that IS a health hazard. But of course, there again it's a matter of *degree*. Churchill was a very heavy drinker, and he lived to be 90. Usually, it's much more of a health hazard than that, of course—it damages the liver.

The point is that people think of just the *advantages* of a career. Like being a movie director: you got all these girls, you've got a house in Hollywood. Sure, you've got all those things! But they don't think about all the headaches, and all the difficulties—the *bad* side! Any profession has its disadvantages, its traps—its boring, annoying, aspects.

Fear of Writing?

Oh, good heavens, *no*. Any irrational fear is pretty, very rare. I don't know... there are all *kinds* of frames of mind once you start writing. Then there's *writer's block*. It's something of an occupational hazard. It's something that comes and goes, and the best I can find I can do is to *do something else. DO* something else, if possible. Or do some simple form of writing like editing, or writing a straightforward essay. Or *something...* It's always deterring for any writer, even if it hangs on for two days! It's one of the occupational hazards of writing—some people never get over it and never write again! Quite a few have been knocked right out of writing.

And when you start writing again—

It's always good, like coming out of any bad experience.

Did you almost become an O.S.S. spy?

Well, as I say, I almost got into the outfit! Had I gotten in... Well, somebody along the line didn't like me. So I didn't get in, but had I gotten in, I don't know *what* would have happened! But I see an affinity with this because there is a very definite affinity between writing and intelligence work: keeping your eyes open, seeing what's going on, seeing whether you've seen *that* person before. You've got to have a tremendous memory for faces and details. All those things are very necessary for a writer, or very *useful* for a writer. So the discipline is not at all dissimilar.

What about medicine?

There is an affinity [between medicine and writing]... I was thinking more of general medicine than specialized...

Did your family ever accept your writing?

No, not at all. Well, it's just one of those things to understand. It's like, you know, you try to converse with your grandmother. I saw that it could be extremely *unpleasant* and very upsetting, so I never showed her at all any of my writing. I know that my mother never did read any of it. Nor did my father. If it's going to upset them, they won't do it. That's all.

In the Brookner film, you revisit your childhood room in St. Louis: was that a powerful experience for you?

Well, not nearly so much as you'd think it might be, because you've been back thousands of times *in your mind!* So when you actually *get* there, there's something anticlimactic about it. [Cat meows loudly in the background] Ohmigod! Oh, you shut up!

So we go back to the house, and the lady doctor in St. Louis was a fan, so she asked us in. I've seen her since. Whenever I go to St. Louis, she invites me over. We came in and photographed the house and garden.

You talked about nightmares and fear of the dark which you experienced in that room. Do you still have that?

No. But it was in that room.

You never benefited from the Burroughs fortune?

No. As I explained, the family was bought off for peanuts long before I was born. There were four of them, and they got about $400,000—that's a hundred thousand each. That block of stock is now worth about six million. So that is that.

If you'd had that Burroughs fortune—

Oh, I'm sure I might *not* have written *Naked Lunch*. Or

probably anything else! Show me a *good* rich writer!

You're writing a book *The Western Lands;* what is the book about?

The Western Lands is an Egyptian paradise, which is reached by a very dangerous road. I speak of this, of course, in *The Place of Dead Roads.* But this is a very clear follow-up on *The Place of Dead Roads.*

Do you get up in the morning and start writing?

I don't have any projected starting time, but I usually get to it about ten o'clock in the morning, after breakfast. If it's going well, I work along until maybe six o'clock. If it isn't going well, I may stop. I may write a few pages, but I don't have any regular schedule.

Talk about your early book, *Junky*—

It holds up for what it *was.* It had very few pretensions. I was just trying to remember what had happened and put it on paper as clearly as I could. That's all. Very simple.

Who do you read?

Oh, well, I don't read a great deal. I read spy stuff, doctor stuff. Spy and doctor books. And horror stories. A lot of spy stuff. Sometimes you get good ideas—the writer has an idea but he can't *develop* it.

Did you have a "classical" education?

No, I wouldn't say "classical" education at *all.* I just had four years of Latin and didn't go on with any classics. No, it was English Literature.

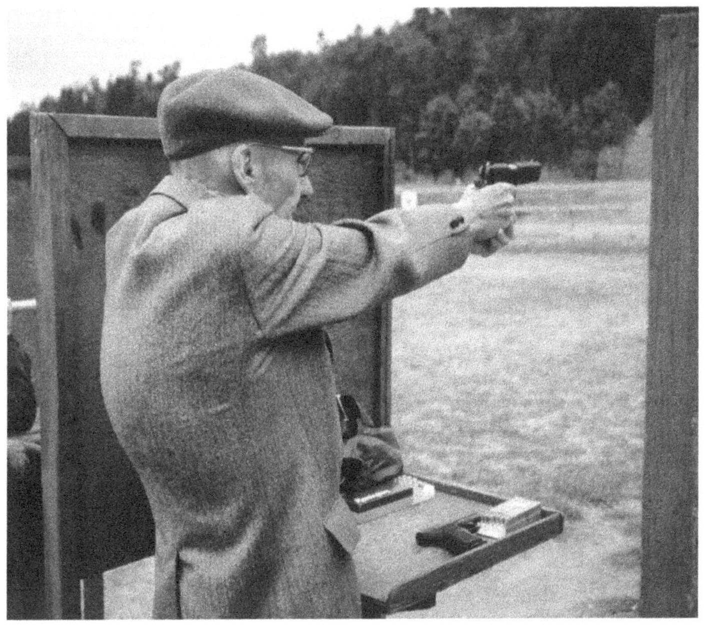

William S. Burroughs at Chabot Range

Did you graduate from Harvard?

Oh, yes.

Do you play chess?

I don't have a mathematical bent of mind at all—can't play chess. In fact, I can't *interest* myself in chess. So no, I'm not that kind of a mind.

Do you still do cut-ups?

Well, I do them occasionally… Come here, little cat.

[Burroughs plays with the cat.]

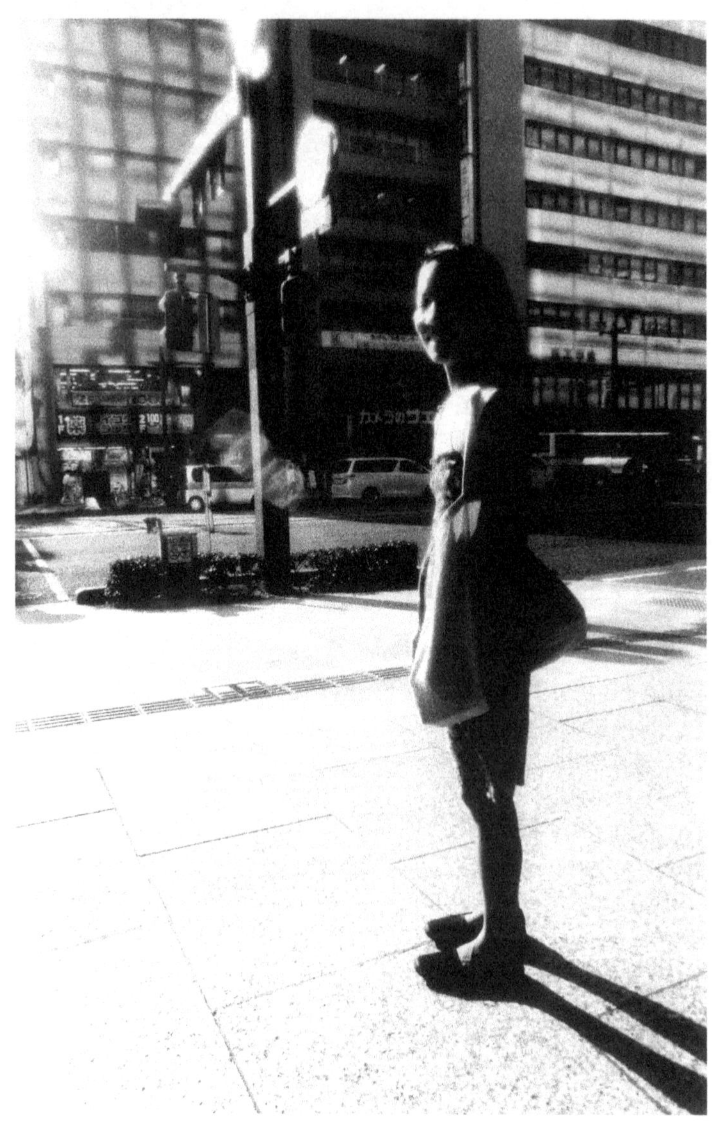

Photo: Yoshi Yubai

WILLIAM S. BURROUGHS: The Final Interview

V. Vale visited Burroughs at his home in Lawrence, Kansas on April 27, 1997. This was Vale's final interview with Burroughs before his death on August 2, 1997. The complete interview appears here for the first time.

William S. Burroughs: How long are you going to be around, Vale?

Vale: I'm leaving in a few hours, William.

Back to San Francisco. How are things there?

We're just working industriously—

That's always good.

I've got a baby daughter.

Do you really? Congratulations!

Thanks. Seventeen months. I brought a picture.

Looks good!

That's the mom and that's the daughter. We're still doing our small press publishing.

[inhales on joint] This stuff is the best anti-nausea drug

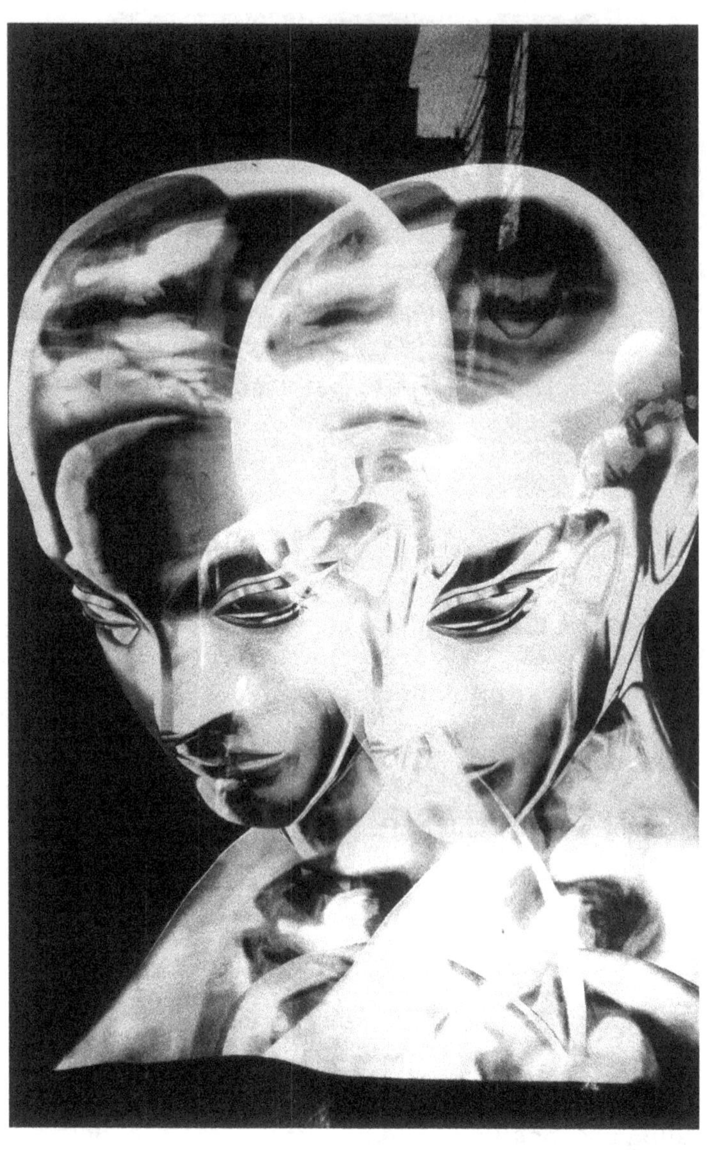

Photo: Yoshi Yubai

there is . . . the *only* one I know of that works. Last time I felt ill I had three puffs and my nausea was gone.

I'm amazed that you can "score" here.

Pot?

Yes.

Well, they *grow* it here. Still got your cats?

I hate to say it, but Lemur died. We had a funeral for him and we even had a tombstone.

What happened to him?

He died of old age. He was a purebred Korat cat and he only lived fourteen years.

They're getting a longer lifespan now. For example, Steven Lowe's Burmese cat—a small cat—lived to be twenty. My cat, Ginger, is about sixteen. You can tell that she's old.

I erected a large tiki that I got at a garage sale as a tombstone, and then we served pie and ice cream. My friend Mindy was there—you went out shooting with him at Chabot in the Oakland Hills many years ago. You had a Korat, didn't you?

I had one [a gift from Peter Weller], but it couldn't get along with the other cats. I kept it for a while, then Steve kept it for a while and it couldn't get along with his cats, and then Udo Breger kept it for a while. It's a one-cat deal, the Korat.

I wanted to get another Korat but the baby kinda threw a spanner in the works. Actually, we had

another cat that you didn't meet: a black-and-white American tabby, kind of scrappy. It's got a girlfriend on the roof next door.

You can't live without a cat.

Russian Blues are very nice cats. They're beautiful, very affectionate. They're described as shy, gentle, sensitive animals that become firmly attached to their owners.

That's important. Korats are very lively, they jump all over—

They're very active. Steve said she's been running all over the house; you can't believe it. She's a speedy little thing, up and down stairs, jumping into couches.

You know what my cat used to do? In my bedroom, when my door would be ajar at an angle, he'd scramble up and perch on top of the door.

Really?

He'd then sit there and look down at me, and eventually—I knew it was coming—he'd leap down.

Onto you.

Yes. But he slept with me every night.

I have two cats that sleep with me. I've got three cats in all, but two that sleep on my bed every night. Sometimes, three. When I turn over, I just push them aside.

[William goes to feed the fish in his backyard pond]

This pond: I don't recall this being so built-up back in '88. It's beautiful. Is that a frog that just hopped

into the pond?

I hope so! We usually have at least three or four frogs in there. It's four-and-a-half or five feet deep. [The workers] cut through all the roots, smoothed it out, and put in a layer of sand and then they put in the liner, sort of thick inner tubes. It's better than concrete, which splits, and it's cheaper. These fish have been here all winter.

There's a lot there; it looks like twenty of them.

At least. They're all colors, from black to white.

They survive the freeze in the winter?

They go into biostasis. You shouldn't feed them then. I've seen fish frozen solid in ice. They come out during the spring. Frozen solid!

What happened to the cats? [looking at tombstones] Calico, Spooner and Ruski died here... Do people come and remove the algae in the pond?

If they don't come in the next day or so, I'll take it out myself. The fish eat the algae, but not that much. We'll have to watch that pond because two times we've found in there a big turtle.

A turtle?

They come from that ditch that's filled up with water. There's sort of a stream there.

They don't eat the fish, though?

They would—if they were in there, of course, they would eat the fish. That's their natural food. They'll eat almost anything. We pulled one out and it was that big around. [gestures about a foot]

I like turtles, though.

A beautiful thing it was. It was black with green spots glistening. Whenever I see one on the road I return it to the nearest water.

The only thing I really can't stand are some insects. The bigger they are, the worse they are. The centipede is an abomination—calls out my genocidal instinct! There ain't room for the both of us in this universe.

[laughs] That's your cat there.

Ginger, the yellow cat. She's getting old, but she gets around. Probably will live another four years. They seem to be living longer—I don't know why.

It's nice and anarchic out here in this yard.

We have some big vegetables out here. But we haven't got a cup of blackberries the whole time we've been here in ten years; I guess the birds get them. We've raised some great tomatoes, and beans and stuff.

That's where you taught me how to throw knives, against that wall. Look at that big black cat!

That's Fletch.

Fletch is still alive?

Is he ever!

He was alive when I was here. Great.

He's about thirteen. It's hard to know. He's probably about twelve or thirteen. When we got him, he was about six months old.

[Looking at fish pond] That white fish has been here at least two years. That big speckled one has been here for years—there it goes! You can see the fossil rock in the pond; it's about five years old.

Do you still have the P7 [a gun]?

Yes, and I have a Glock now.

How do you like it?

I like the Glock. It's very reliable, I think.

There's such a publicity campaign that I've rarely seen. You can't open up a gun magazine without a picture of a Glock shoved down your throat.

They have so many models now. They added a .45. As I recall, you didn't like the Glock.

I didn't. Fred had one, and it was shaving off pieces of plastic. And another thing about it is: the two-trigger thing confused me, and I couldn't even hit the target with it. I probably just didn't get used to it—so many people can't be wrong!

I still prefer a double-action revolver.

So do I; I'm a revolver man. For one thing, automatics are much more trouble to clean. Yes, I stick with revolvers.

They don't have any magazine spring to weaken over time.

Uh, well, automatics are reliable now. Jesus Christ, that

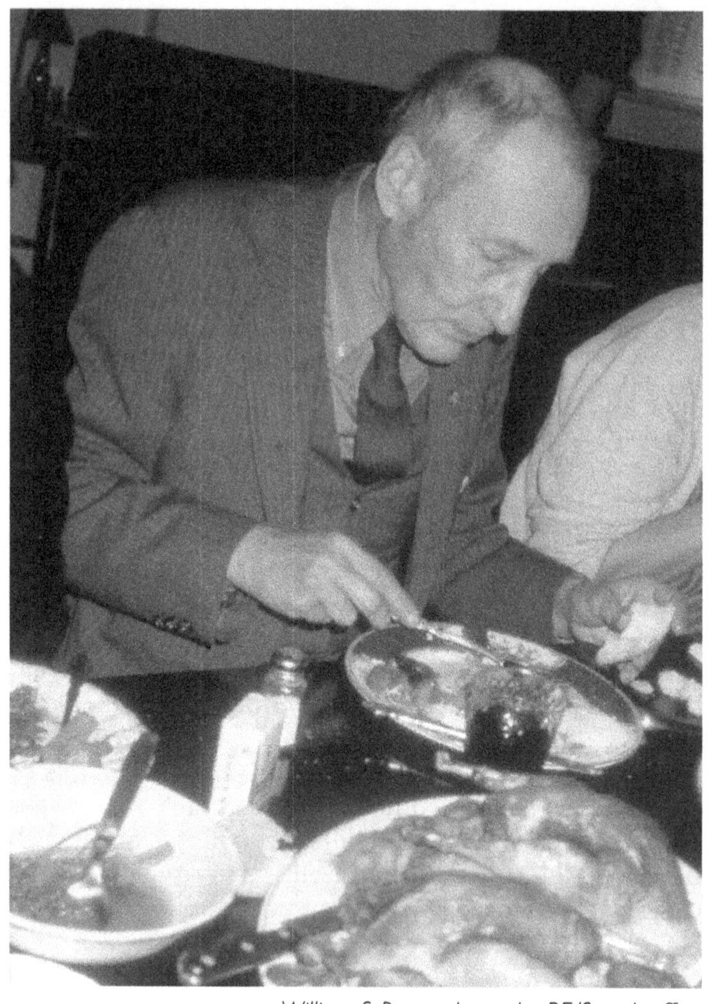

William S. Burroughs at the RE/Search office

old .45 I've had for about damn near fifteen years... haven't had any trouble with it, and it was second-hand when I got it.

You would never be arrested around here, William, for having guns.

Oh, no; this is gun country. The governor vetoed the concealed-weapon law here, but I wouldn't hesitate to carry one anyway—I *don't* hesitate to carry one anyway; what the hell. Very little will happen, actually: you wouldn't go to jail or anything like that. [feeds fish] Okay, this is the last you're going to get.

What happens if you overfeed them?

Nothing. A goldfish is really just a carp, basically.

William, I read your statement in the *New York Times* about Allen Ginsberg dying. That was a big shock to me; he's the person who gave me money to start publishing—he was a big help to me. I finally wanted to do something with my life and wanted to do a publication on what I thought was the next social revolution, Punk Rock. I asked him about it and he said, "Of course I know Punk Rock; I've been to CBGB's; I know Patti Smith." And without even asking, he whipped out his checkbook and wrote me a check for a hundred dollars. That was a lot of money back then; it was like half a month's salary for me.

He gave so much money away, did so many things to help people.

I don't know if many people are aware that he gave people like me money.

He liked to introduce people to other people. There are some people who don't. I used to call them pimps and anti-pimps. There is a whole class of people who like to separate people; they don't like to see anyone else get together, even though they have no stake in the matter. They're anti-pimps. Or anti-Venus.

Allen was very calm about the whole thing [his impending death]. The doctors told him, "You've got two to four months." And Allen said, "I think much less." He told me, "I thought I'd be terrified waiting for the diagnosis, but I'm not. I'm exhilarated!" I've heard other people say the same thing: instead of being terrified, they're sort of *liberated,* somehow.

I would like to be that way!

Well, maybe you will. "I thought I'd be terrified, but I'm not—I'm exhilarated!"—those were his *very words.* See, I talked to him the day before he died, and that was what he said.

Before that I called the hospital—he's always in and out of hospitals. He said, "Well, the doctors are taking tests. They're trying to decide whether it's hepatitis or jaundice. They don't know what kind of hepatitis it is, so they have to make more tests. They have a passion for tests." The sound of his voice was bad then, very weak—it sounded like a very serious illness. It was just a few days later he called up to say that it was inoperable liver cancer and that he had two to four months at most.

Well, they always give the best possible prognosis. Sometimes they're wrong one way and sometimes they're wrong another. In fact, with Stephen Lowe's mother, they had her dead three years before she died. She had bone cancer, which is very painful, but they have a hospice here. They have a chair in which they just have to press a button, and they get morphine. She never felt any pain as far as I could see.

Occasionally she'd run her machine dry or something, and Stephen would have to take her over to the emergency room. And they all knew them and immediately gave her a shot of morphine. They knew she had terminal cancer; none of this nonsense of withholding; what the hell are painkillers for if not for people *in pain?* For Christ's sake!

Here they are, waking up to that fact now. So that's a case for morphine, or heroin if that doesn't work.

You see, quantitative differences, at a certain point, become *qualitative.* For example, codeine is a good painkiller at the lower levels, but there's pain that no amount of codeine would alleviate, but which can be relieved by morphine. There's pain that cannot be relieved by morphine that can be relieved by Dilaudid or heroin. So a quantitative difference becomes *qualitative* at a certain point.

So morphine and heroin is as good as it gets?

Well, they're still not manufacturing heroin here—I don't know why. It's manufactured in England, France, and most of Europe; it's a better painkiller than morphine—it's less nauseating. So it has a lot of advantages over morphine, and it takes a smaller quantity to alleviate pain. Dilaudid is somewhere between morphine and heroin. It's actually a dehydrated chemical variation of morphine. It's not a synthetic; Demerol or Methadone are pure synthetics, just as good.

For god's sake, when you start talking about someone of his or her *age,* with terminal cancer: "He might become an addict!" Holy shit! What could be more ridiculous? Some people have some religious idea; I remember this one doctor here in Lawrence asked this woman, "Well, you wouldn't want your father to die *addicted,* would you?!" Ridiculous.

It's funny, I was thinking on the way over here that the Ten Commandments are not enough!

They sure aren't! They're very inadequate.

And that should be one of them, "Thou shalt not withhold pain relief from the suffering. Thou shalt

not be homophobic. Thou shalt not be racist."

These people are in great pain that's not being relieved because they're not getting enough morphine. And then, in fear of this pain going on, they ask for assisted suicide. I'm not in favor of assisted suicide at all. In the first place, if those people had the proper hospice care, they wouldn't have this fear, they wouldn't have this pain.

What's that rule: Love thy neighbor as thyself—

You see, it's getting to the point that you hate him because he *is* your neighbor, with this overpopulation. Here you are, you just got room enough for yourself, and somebody will *plonk* down here—and he's your neighbor even if you don't like it!

Here there are all sorts of complicated situations. The whole question of genocide. All sorts of—

What's the Golden Rule—do you remember it?

Of course: "Do unto others as you would have them do unto you." The trouble is that tastes differ: "Do others before they do you."

I read in an Allen Ginsberg interview: "Be as wise as serpents and as gentle as doves."

Oh yes, that's an old Chinese saying—I think it goes back to Taoism. That's a very, very profound philosophy, Taoism. There's a great deal of wisdom in Confucius too, *migod.* There was a joke in the *New Yorker:* "Papa's tired; tell Mama what Confucius say." There was a lot of "Confucius Say" nonsense back in the Thirties.

Everybody's life is so unique, it's a tricky thing to

try and come up with universal laws.

Also, there are too many everybodys! This goes back to the Industrial Revolution. They want more and more people to work in their factories and buy their products. People have learned now that this is a liability—a deadly liability and a dangerous liability: all these ignorant stupid people.

And what makes them ignorant and stupid? I think it's because they're getting all their information from television.

Well, the old factories, I think: aren't they sort of *folding?* General Motors—of course, they produce a certain amount which they can immediately sell. But in the old days they would be able to absorb huge numbers of unemployed workers—unemployed unskilled workers. The tendency now seems to be toward fewer unskilled workers and a lot of automation, and the computer is taking over. So there are lots of useless people out there living on welfare mostly, or on benefits.

I drive through parts of San Francisco, and there are lots of unemployed men just standing around on the sidewalk.

Well, there are all sorts of angles. One thing is their unemployment benefits and all that.

Have you ever read anything by this psychologist (one of the few psychologists who makes any sense) M. Scott Peck. He wrote *The Road Less Traveled,* and now he's written another book called *The Denial of the Soul.* The last one is very good. Like me, he believes in God! He thinks most psychologists deny the one vital thing: the soul. He's very much opposed to euthanasia, and he says that a lot of that of course is fear of pain. This is ridiculous because they don't have hospices available here.

But he says that dying is an *experience,* and to duck this means that you're depriving yourself of a great spiritual experience. He's very good, very sound. I'd recommend the book very highly.

For me the biggest shock that I've been under is the fact that Allen died; it's been a month.

Well, it didn't bother *him!* A lot of people have reported this exhilaration in the near-death experience.

It was also sad losing Lemur. Lemur was on your lap once.

Oh I remember; a cute little thing. It was lying in the middle of the floor and I picked it up. God, I just love cats. Beautiful things.

[William goes somewhere and looks for an issue of *Connoisseur* magazine with an article on Singapura cats ("the most beautiful cats").]

There was a song by the [San Francisco] Mutants called "The New Dark Ages": "We're living in the New Dark Ages."

It is amazing how driven humans are by sex...

Oh, well, I don't think so. Mostly they're driven by sex because it's been *suppressed* more than anything else. Otherwise, it would be sort of a casual thing, as it is in many primitive societies. It's more important as a sociological factor than as an individual psychological thing. In most of these societies, there may be a matriarchal lineage that emphasizes the female sex—that is that the possessions are passed down the female line. Or it may be patrilineal—all this sort of stuff. The sociological aspects of the position of the sexes in this society…

People in the Highlands of New Guinea: I don't think they have that attitude. They feel it's a simple thing, part of their life. I think we've gotten *that* invasive attitude by our sort of *fear* of it, our aversion: "*Ohmigod,* this is a terrible, terrible thing. My grandmother says she just read a book that mentioned homosexuality… things you didn't know *existed!"* That meant they were absolutely terrible, if you didn't know they existed. That's the first step of *unreason* there: the fact that you didn't know these things existed, made them unspeakable. They didn't even have *words* to describe such things.

One of the big issues of anthropology is this pregnancy thing. Some people have said that there's no connection between sexual intercourse and pregnancy. They say that, but they know better. This anthropologist does not realize that when someone says something, it may not be anything he believes *at all.* It's like doublethink, you know. There are so many things that people know and don't quite know that they know. Like people on the seacoast in the Middle Ages goddamn well knew the earth was round! But they pretended to believe. It was *healthier* to believe that the earth was flat, because the Church said so! They had that *social pressure,* although still in their minds they knew it was round. And *Jesus Christ,* in New Guinea they knew that there was a connection between fucking and pregnancy.

I think our sexuality is screwed up by too many media images inundating us, which provoke us sexually.

I've never had that trouble. I don't see it that way. *Your images come from yourself, I feel.* My images come from myself: "That is the type of person that I'm attracted to." In Tangier, I liked this type of Arab or that type of Spanish boy, and so on, but I didn't feel that the media got in my way at all. I don't care what they say/think. All they got

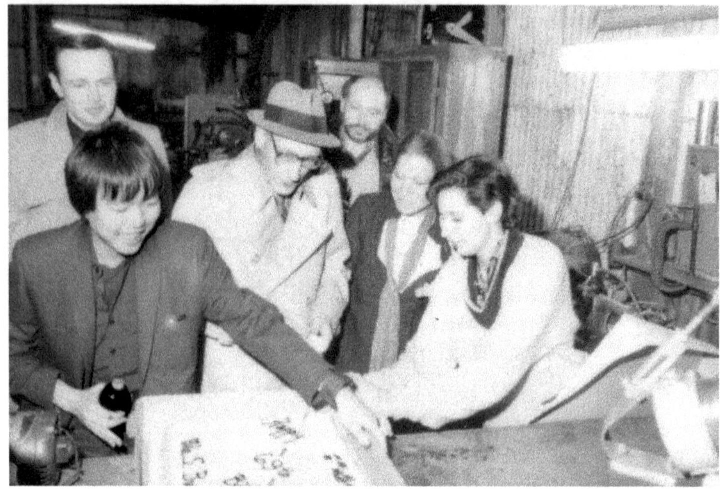

William S. Burroughs with V. Vale and friends at Survival Research Labs

is *cunts, cunts, cunts!* Jesus Christ! Sticking their *tits* out at you, and their *cunts* rotating up in your face—shit man, I don't need that. I don't mind; it's all right for them that likes it. I don't!

You watch TV fairly regularly, right?

Well, if there's something on it. I saw a great program on the meerkats. They aren't cats at all, they're mongooses. Oh, they were so great, those meerkats. They're the cutest things I've almost ever seen. There's a classic picture of one standing up like this with a little tiny one down here—it's incredible. I've got a picture here where an eagle grabbed the young meerkat. The meerkat went right up—it was a male—and attacked the eagle. It lunged for the eagle; it could break its leg easily—and the eagle dropped the meerkat and flew away. And the meerkat wasn't hurt.

I've got a lot of animal books showing pictures of all these different animals. I'm such a great animal lover. It's such a piece of yourself. I feel a cat is a piece of myself—that's why it hurts so much when they die. You're losing a piece of yourself that used to be there. Yes, Wordsworth, in his Lucy poem: "She died and left me, this sea, this calm, this quiet scene, in memory of what has been and nevermore will be."

Do you ever feel like you're harmed by watching television, ever?

Well, I don't watch it. [laughs] Oh no, I'm never harmed by watching television. I watch something like that: a natural history program. I'm *glad* to have that.

[William gets a cortisone eyedrop; he leans back] I had a cataract operation a week ago, and *migod* what a great thing! I was getting so I could hardly read, and now my vision is almost normal.

That's a miracle!

I know, it's a fucking miracle! I met someone else that I knew: an old shooting buddy of mine. When I went in for the operation, and then I saw him the next day in the doctor's office: we both had huge patches on our eyes. He had his patch removed. So the doctor did two [operations] in one day; it's pretty cut-and-dried. He has a laser thing; it takes about an hour, and I felt none of it. If they gave me any anesthetic, I didn't feel anything.

They gave me a little Valium or something, and I didn't hardly feel it. So then, there he is at my head, down there. He had immobilized the eye some way, but I felt nothing. I could feel him, every now and then, squirting some water or something against the eye, and then feel him reaching in there, *buzzzzzzz,* that's it, y'know. But it was completely painless. I was there for about half an hour chatting with the nurses, and—I don't know; I should have done it long ago!

He was telling me, "Listen, you're gonna find..." (You see, I'd been there several times) "You're gonna get to a point where you can't read." And I finally decided, "By god, this one day or the next, I'm gonna do it." It was so easy; I called him on Wednesday; he told me to come in for lab work at Lawrence Memorial; be there either Thursday or Friday. I went Thursday; he said, "The operation will be done on Monday." I said, "Well, Jesus, this is fast work." I was afraid it would be "two months from now" and all that kind of crap, but it wasn't at all. I called him and less than a week later I had the operation. Doctor Orchard; he's good.

The procedure's getting more standardized. The cornea: they take the lens out and put a plastic lens in; I don't know how they get the right shape or anything! But I felt almost no discomfort at any time. At first, it felt sort of like something's a little bit in your eye, but nothing. And I have to take eyedrops for about another week, but that's all right. There's cortisone, and antibiotics, both (plus a special saline solution). I have to sit down and get my head back or I don't know where the fuck it is—gonna put drops all over my face! I wouldn't say there have been too many "misses"—there've been a couple. But the only way I can control that is to get my head all the way around, and it works pretty well.

That was a week ago?

Three or four days later, I suddenly found overnight that I could read.

What are you reading?

I'm reading a book called *Extinct.* It seems that one of these great white sharks that is a hundred feet long has survived somewhere, and now it's eaten some boys, just for starters. It's gonna eat some more. Someone found a tooth about as long as that [demonstrates]. "It's been extinct for five million years": That's what YOU think!

I never asked you this, but did you ever read those old *Doc Savage* books in the '30s?

Some of them. Did *you* ever read the *Fu Manchu* books?

I love those!

Oh, man: "Fu Manchu: then he sought the *source* of opium." He was so evil, you see—he was so "the East"; the whole East was described as evil and devious in soul, and the West was frank and straightforward and *decent*—good god! "The Egyptian delegate looked more like a beautiful evil woman than a man."

There were consummate evil people in *Fu Manchu.* Those were funny! A guy sticks his head out the window and some guy, a dacoit on the roof, whips a noose around his neck and threw him out the window! Another guy's down by the river and here he sees a duck sailing placidly by, turns his back, and a knife whizzes by. He turns around and realizes there's a dacoit under the duck!

The *Doc Savage* books are full of amazing ways to kill people, and hypnotic gases—

Migod, yes. Fu Manchu had what he called the "Red Bride"—it was this red centipede. He'd send a letter, and this had a scent that attracted this thing. He'd let it down a chimney on a string and then it'd go and kill the guy. The Red Bride, he called it: "How many of the Red Brides do we have left?"

That's brilliant: the deadly centipede attracted by the scent from a letter.

The *insidious Doctor Fu Manchu.*

He cranked out quite a few of those.

Sax Rohmer was the *Fu Manchu* guy. "Sax" is some fake name; his real name was Jerry Finkelstein or something. The other guy was H. Rider Haggard—he's the one who did *She.* Every time she put up her hands to get more "use" she got older. She lived so long that I'm surprised she had the strength left to scuttle off, offstage, like a dying beetle! There was also *King Solomon's Mines.* This old crone was saying, "There they are; eat of them and drink of them." This door was closing, gonna starve them all to death! They found another exit and got out some way, and the old hag got crushed.

I just started reading the *Doc Savage* novels.

I don't think I ever encountered those. I read *Black Mask;* I remember *Weird Tales* and *Amazing Stories*—there were some very good ones in there, and some of them I've never been able to find. I used some of those in my own work, but I'd like to find the originals, but never could. Who was that guy [who wrote about] "the Old Ones"?

H.P. Lovecraft?

There was somebody else.

Arthur Machen?

He was another one, too. But anyway, Lovecraft was quite good and earnest. This place right by the—it's always in New England—where there's vile rural slums that stunk of fish because they're these half-fish people! It was great.

Did you ever read a book called *Waiting For Nothing* by Tom Kromer (it came out in 1935, during the Depression)?

I don't know it.

It was a memoir of the Great Depression. He's always trying to turn to crime, but he doesn't quite have the guts to pull off a bank robbery because the gun got caught in the lining of his coat.

He never *does* anything?

He wants to hit someone over the head with a club and steal his wallet but when it comes down to it he can't do it. But it's still pretty stark. Chapter three or four has a homosexual encounter, which was pretty daring for its time.

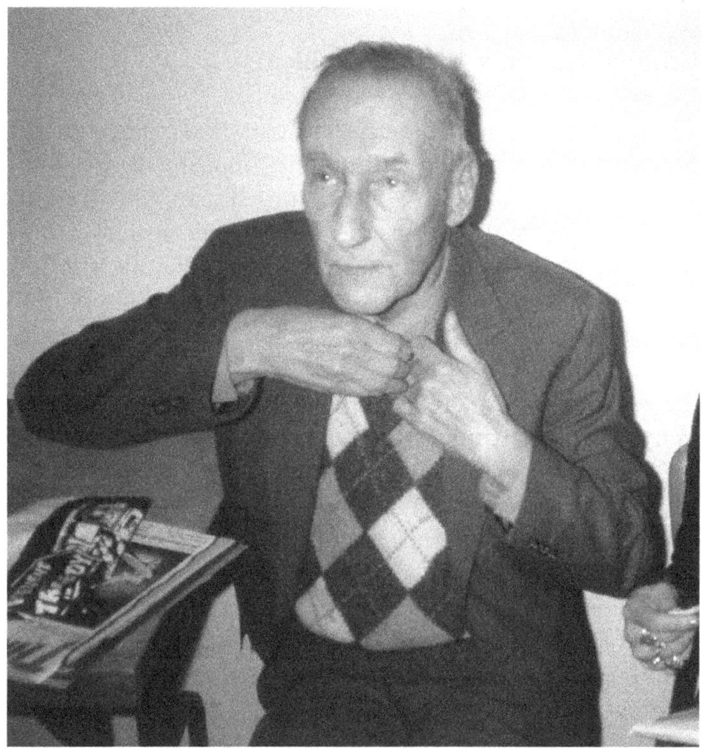

William S. Burroughs in San Francisco

I know when I had to hit someone or kick him in the ribs, I *did* it.

It was part of a genre called proletarian novels. They're mostly written during the Depression.

Some of it is *fake proletarian,* from the old Communist Party line: [sings] "All the workers had to stand in line for a lousy dollar a day/And down in Harlan County, there are neutrals there/You'll either be a union man/Or scrounge for J.H. Blair." [song is "Which Side Are You On?" by Pete Seeger; original by Florence Reece] And this is all phony—phony, cooked-up Communist bile: "Oh, you can't scare me; I'm sticking to the unions."

I thought unions had their place.

They pushed a lot of people out of their place to get there. But really, if a plumber is making more than an assistant professor, they certainly can't beef about what they're making now. The most reactionary group in America is the so-called working class: construction workers and people like that. The most homophobic and the most fascist-oriented people are the working-class, so-called.

Why do you suppose that happened?

I'll tell you how it happened. The workers got guys like this in there to organize them, and they got more and more money until they were fucking making more money than most people. They were right up there in the salary range of the white-collar class. It's pretty simple how they got there: Hoffa. But that whole political stuff doesn't interest me very much.

There are certainly a lot of people right now having

a hard time surviving, especially young people. In San Francisco, the rents there have gone up at least ten times.

Everywhere. The redwoods and cedars along the coast of California—we went there—land there has gone out of sight. Beautiful country there: redwood and cedar.

Seismically things have been okay, just little tremors.

That's bad for the tourist business; bad for real estate investment: the fucking San Andreas fault, or whatever they call it. It isn't good.

I think everybody has amnesia these days. They've already forgotten about that '89 earthquake.

Well, that's just as well!

One of my ideas is that people's memories are growing worse and worse because of overwhelming input from television.

That's partly it, but certainly memories are getting absolutely worse in a way that makes you wonder. High school graduates: two-thirds of them had no idea who our Allies were in the Second World War. They all knew the name of Hitler, but Roosevelt was, of course, *Teddy* Roosevelt. And as for Churchill—they all drew a blank. As to finding where France and England and where the war was fought on the map—no idea! It's just appalling.

What do you attribute this to?

I don't know. It's mysterious, it's very sinister. It's like they've been blanked out. It's very sinister. These statistics are upsetting. Half or thirty percent, or something like that, thought that two people who had homosexual intercourse could contract AIDS, even though neither of them was infected by the virus—the immaculate conception, my dear? God Almighty! Where are their *heads?*

[After a gap in conversation] Judges always side with the arresting officers—well, not always, by any means. They've really cracked down heavy on fraudulent convictions. They use informants now. You remember that bit that happened in Boston last year?

No.

Well, there was this retired minister who was sixty-nine years old with heart trouble. So the cops bust in, kick the door down, throw him on the floor, cuff him behind his back—all of this. He dies of a heart attack. Now it turns out that they got the wrong address from an informer. So everybody was embarrassed, believe me. They had to give huge compensation to his widow; she got a big chunk of money. There was another one, like the guy in California on this big ranch. You hear that one?

No.

You're talking about short memories now.

I don't always read the paper.

I read the paper every day. This guy was a rich man who owned a big piece of property, like two hundred acres. And the feds got some deal on him; some warrant that he was growing marijuana. They come in the door in the middle of the night. He walks out with a gun in his hand, and they shoot him and kill him. There was no evidence that he was growing anything; in fact, he was against the whole drug thing. It turned out that the feds wanted this particular piece of property for some reason.

Man, it's so rank! And Ruby Ridge and Waco—they are a bunch of *thugs!* I've lost all confidence in the government. Particularly Ruby Ridge: of course, the government shells out three million dollars; the family was awarded three million dollars. They admit that something happened there that wasn't quite right.

I think they just print the money.

Oh, don't be silly! Of course they *had* to award them the money. They had to do it; of course they gave them that money. If they hadn't . . . *migod,* the climate would have been horrific! It was bad enough in Ruby Ridge, anyway, when they shoot a mother with a baby in her arms for no good reason. So three million dollars was the least they could do!

[Randy Weaver] hadn't *done* anything. They finagled him into taking two inches off a shotgun, thereby making it illegal. This is a very minor infraction. For something that might call for a slight fine, they have this military contingent closing in on the place, shooting his son! This is not reasonable. For years this has been going on!

Ruby Ridge was absolutely uncalled for. To have this huge military maneuver come in there for this very minor infraction for having illegally sawed two inches off the end of a shotgun? Sure, he was a pain in the ass and a white supremacist and all that, but why go through with getting him to commit a minor offense? Nobody knew the feds were there. His son was out there, one of the feds shot the son's dog, the son then shot the fed and then another fed killed the son. This is their opening, just like in Waco. They don't announce themselves; they just walk in. He was waiting to surrender, and they didn't come. His wife was standing in the door with a baby in her arms and was shot and killed by a sniper. Finally, they did come in and take him. And then they had the nerve to try and charge him with killing the fed that was killed in the fight, and the guy was immediately acquitted . . . There are very precise accounts of Ruby Ridge and they all show that the F.B.I. was absolutely and completely out of line.

Once they seized things from me because there was a young jerk in the car that had one joint on him. This is a full-scale fascist government in operation. What can we do? What can any individual do? Let's face it: the Age of the Barricades is over, where you just go out and start putting up a barricade here and there. They got all the guns; they'll drop a few bombs on us or something.

In the marijuana operations in Northern California they do that.

A fortified position counts as a fort and can be knocked out with artillery. So your fortress becomes a death trap as they're raining bombs in there; they're dropping them down and raining them down from the sky.

Did you see this film *The Trigger Effect?* It was about what would happen in a prolonged blackout in which credit cards become useless and no one has any cash. In one scene, this guy is frantically trading his Rolex watch for a cheap shotgun and a box of shells.

For a cheap shotgun?

Yeah.

For drugs! For drugs! He trades the cheap shotgun and the shells for junk—one shot. *Mainline.*

The war against drugs. What a fucking stupid farce, man. What an *evil* farce, because everybody *knows* it's bullshit. Here we have a completely harmless and very beneficent substance: cannabis. They're bearing down on that heavier than they are on heroin.

And crack.

Marijuana: there's no reason for it to be illegal in the first place. And all drugs come from plants, like opium. I've been trying for years to find out what the yield is on opium poppies. The best article ever written on opium is in the old *Encyclopedia Britannica.* I don't know the yield-per-acre or anything. Do you get one shot out of two acres?! The poppies come to, and there's a certain way and a certain time they go out and make incisions in all the poppies. Then they go around and catch the gum that comes out and put that into a cauldron of water they've got ready that's all heated up. They can do it in the

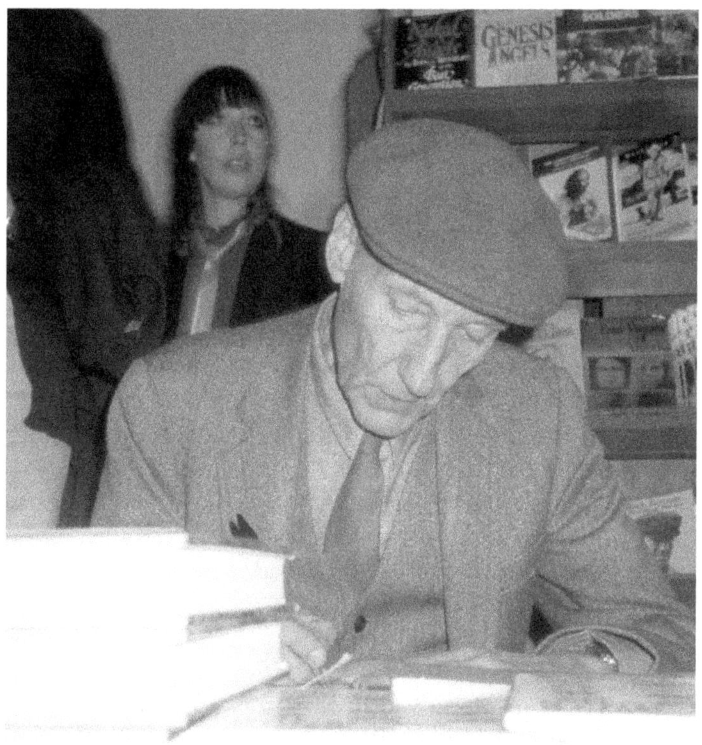

William S. Burroughs at City Lights, San Francisco

evening, in the morning, as long as something's coming out, and then they all use the husks to make a sort of low-grade opium, for workers and people like that.

True Hallucinations—I've got that book in the other room. Terence McKenna. People must have sometimes gone around and tried various plants and found that some had this effect, and some had that, but often guided by the plant itself—the *spirit* of the plant. There are lots of societies which are almost entirely carnivorous, like the Eskimos. But they live on eating the *whole* of the animal: all the blubber and the intestines and the blood and everything. But they suddenly crack right up and die at the age of sixty.

Does anyone eat the giant centipedes?

I hope not, but I have a horrible feeling that at one time there was. I have seen this picture in the Peabody Museum of a guy strapped to a couch, and this giant centipede about six feet long is rearing up in front of him. They said, "Oh, it's just the superstitions of these backward people." But these backward people never had any science fiction! They never had any horror stories. What they portray on there they must have *seen,* somewhere, somehow. That's what I'm talking about; they must have *seen* it. A giant centipede it was, it was sort of reared up—odious! If there's one thing I hate in this universe it's a fucking centipede. More than anything else. I love lizards, I love turtles, I love snakes, but I draw the line at the insects. Well, one insect I have great respect for is the flea. They can jump a mile, did you know that?

No.

They can jump a mile! *God,* they can withstand tons of pressure—they're a magnificent, magnificent beast!

Do you like the gaboon viper?

Well, I don't want one. I saw one; Dean had one. They've got a big poison sac under here, and it growls—it growls like a dog! I had it right on that sofa. [Burroughs growls] It growled like a dog, I swear to god. On my scout's honor, it growled like a dog.

In the San Diego Zoo I saw a snake I liked: a beautiful six-foot-long green tree snake.

Another thing, most snakes do this thing [demonstrates] to propel themselves. But the gaboon viper walks on its ribs—it walks on its fucking ribs, I tell you. They say a bite from a gaboon viper will make a man—this one guy suffered one disability after another after he'd been bitten by a gaboon viper. They're a thick snake; *thick*—from Gaboon, Africa.

I think some perhaps beneficent, perhaps diabolical ark should be sent out to put all of these different species from—say, snakes from Australia—to wherever they could live in North America. The hourglass spider, the only deadly spider, would thrive in Florida, and so on. Of course, some of them would be beneficent; some would be harmful.

What an idea: a malevolent ark. What about sea snakes?

The sea serpents; the sea snakes, are very deadly. The yellow-bellied sea snake has very deadly venom, although they don't ordinarily bite people. But there's the Portuguese man-o'-war jellyfish. They even have an anti-venom for it but it's usually too late; it's so quick. So quick and so painful. Then, hmm...

When I was in Mexico I visited an alligator breeding

farm, or was it a crocodile?

Well, they are different—not too much. I think the crocodile has a longer snout and it can move in some way that the alligator can't. There have been very few alligator attacks, whereas, of course, in Africa and places like that, the crocodiles are a source of considerable casualties. People think that if they're standing on a bank they're perfectly safe there—they're not. You know that a crocodile can move thirty-five miles an hour for a short distance: *Whoa!*

What other poisonous snakes are there? The tiger snake, the death adder, the brown snake, the yellow-bellied sea snake, the blue-ringed octopus—this is a little tiny octopus about as big as an ashtray, absolutely deadly venom. Australia's just crawling with all these deadly things. The funneling spider; a fairly big spider that gets in bathrooms and things. They have very powerful jaws that can punch right through rubber gloves; people have been known to die within twenty minutes. It's the only deadly spider in the world. Of course, people can die from a brown recluse, but *this* is something that's as deadly as a poisonous snake. They have such an efficient way of dealing with bites that they have very few casualties. The First Aid instructions are just: don't do anything, just wrap a tight bandage around it. Then they send a helicopter out and take you to the nearest hospital.

You ever go out fishing, Vale?

Never. You enjoy that?

I *used* to enjoy it, but not anymore. I'm more and more disinclined to kill *any* sentient creature. But I got to draw the line. A psychoanalyst of my acquaintance said about the centipede: "It is frightful! They have no feelings!" It's true; there's no way that you could relate to this horrible thing. There's no way.

I've met a lot of people like that.

There's always something. *Jesus Christ,* you can relate to a cat or a rat—particularly to a meerkat, but you cannot relate to a god... damned... centipede! I can't, can you? Try it. Give it a shot right now. I can't do it. I just hate the things.

Don't you think they're all extinct now?

Oh no. No, no. They're everywhere! Like scorpions: scorpions are one of the most widespread things that there is! In Iceland you find them; *everywhere* there's fucking scorpions! Centipedes are not nearly as prevalent.

It's great to see you again, Vale.

Thank you very much. I like your coat; it has so many pockets.

You have promises to keep, and miles to go before you sleep.

Well, William, I'm so happy to have seen you—

We'll see each other again.

[Note: we never did see each other again!]

◆ ◆ ◆

DIANE DI PRIMA: The Healing Machine

V. Vale interviewed Diane di Prima at her home in 2005. Throughout the past eight decades, Diane di Prima has been a source of inspiration and instruction to hundreds of students and thousands of lovers of poetry—not to mention feminist historians, chroniclers of the so-called "Beat Generation," and anyone seeking humor, wisdom and alternative role models. In this excerpt, di Prima discusses her experience getting to know William S. Burroughs during their time teaching at Naropa.

Diane di Prima: What about Bill at Naropa?

Vale: What did William Burroughs teach there—*Creative Writing?*

di Prima: I don't remember what he taught. We taught ourselves. We taught how to free your mind and do what you want. I went to his performance lectures, but I don't think I went to any of his classes. But I remember that we were in this—I wrote about this—there was a little piece that they did at Bill's memorial at the S.F. Art Institute. I wasn't in town, but they taped me ahead of time for it.

I remember a séance we went to together. He wasn't the organizer of it—that was a woman who was a poet and a friend of Robert Duncan's; a woman named Helen Luster. Bill was invited, I was invited, some other people

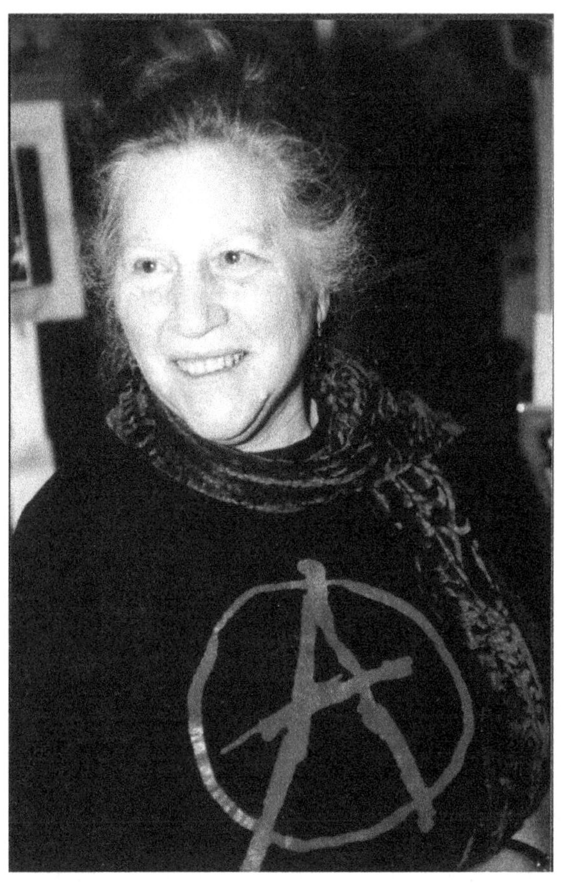

were invited. People were sitting around—I mean, this was New Age bullshit: nothing's happening here! And Bill stood up, went to a certain spot in this small Naropa apartment (we were all given these tiny little student quarters) and he said, "We have to erect a column of light—right here!" and pointed to a place. I don't know what other people got. He and I got a lot of stuff, and compared notes somewhat later, and so on.

So he and I had a bond on the level of magical work and stuff, but he didn't talk about it with too many people;

I didn't know if he talked about it with you much. Like, when I would visit him at his house, sometimes he would show me… he had these 19th-century books about pulling energy from the atmosphere for healing—stuff like that. (And there's one of them I'd really like to get, but I don't remember its title, though so I can't tell you—sorry! I have it written down.)

He would show me, like, a healing machine that he was working with. He would put the photo of who he wanted to work on in this thing and it was a contraption built to draw power down and direct it at this person through the connection of their photograph. And he said, "You know, it's much easier to heal animals than people, because they don't have any resistance. They have no hidden agenda that keeps them from wanting to be healed… the way humans do." And he was so tender about that.

I saw Bill as incredibly, incredibly tender, and horribly intelligent, as you know—so intelligent that it must have been hard to be around people. All of that would disappear, including any of our kind of talk, as soon as another person would enter the room. He would be pretending to be drunk and saying clownish stupid things, and trying on hats. And people would go, "Oh, that Bill… What a joker."

But, I really think he was the heart of that whole crowd. He was the heart and soul of Allen, Jack, Gregory, all those people… who by the way, were a very small piece of what the Beat movement was. Or what was going on—I don't know if you want to call it the Beat movement.

I think you can call it the Beat movement if you can think of the Beat movement as a kind of, like, communal effort to expand the boundaries of what goes in the arts and what goes in consciousness. If you limit it to anything else, then that's bullshit because there are so many kinds of—I mean, is the San Francisco Renaissance included or not? What about the Black Mountain people? They start splintering it all up. But, it was *one* thing that was going on. And Gregory, Allen, and so on, are one part of it, but they were the ones who liked to get publicity and get out there that way. So that's the group that everyone thinks is the whole thing. And they were my friends and I love them, but they were only a *piece* of this whole thing—there were many other things going on!

They all were thrusting in the same direction: How far can you push the envelope in the arts? How far can you push it in consciousness? What are the frontiers? Where can we *really go* with the mind? What is the mind willing to do? It's infinite; we have this infinite tool at our disposal. And we were in a period where we were willing to, like, push the boundaries of it. And now, people are so scared, it's ridiculous. But you know, Bill and all that—that was part of it.

◆ ◆ ◆

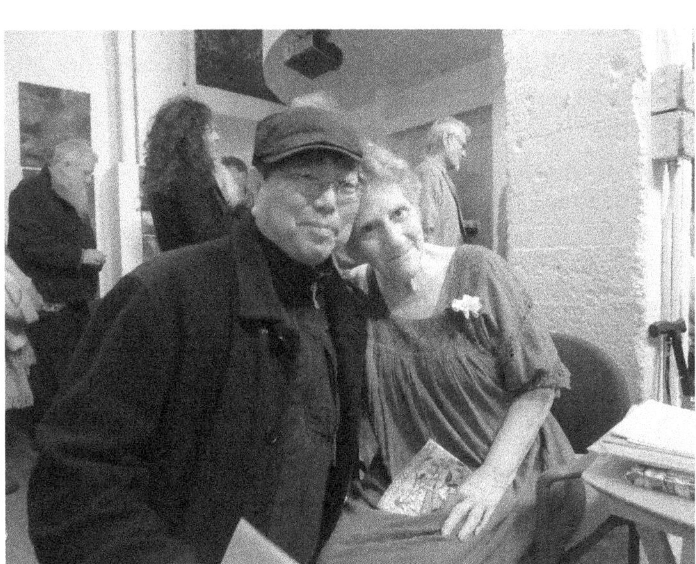

Diane di Prima's birthday celebration at Emerald Tablet

GERALD V. CASALE: "Too Many People!"

In 1982, Devo founder Gerald V. Casale did a legendary interview with William S. Burroughs for Trouser Press *magazine. In this interview with V. Vale, Casale talks about his experience conducting this interview. This interview was videotaped for RE/Search's* The Counterculture Hour *on public access television, San Francisco.*

Vale: We're extremely happy to have Gerald V. Casale, one of the founding philosophers, theoreticians and idea-people behind the band DEVO…Can you tell us about meeting William Burroughs back in the eighties?

Gerald V. Casale: Somebody at *Trouser Press* magazine in New York City had the idea of sending Mark [Mothersbaugh] and I to interview William Burroughs but he said, "No, I want to interview THEM." We went to his bunker in New York City that had been some kind of boys' locker room or something, or the showers—it was windowless—and he showed us his guns, and his cane that has a retractable switchblade that comes out the bottom, so for us… we had our *poses,* as the edgy artists who took ourselves seriously… but after about fifteen minutes of being at William Burroughs' place, **we'd already been reduced to, like, high-school freshmen that'd just met a hardcore beatnik!**

We were really put in our place, and then the real fun started. We explained our ideas about de-evolution, and he was mildly amused… and then he retorted [imitates Burroughs's Midwestern drawl], "Really, Jerry, **the problem is: there's just too many people on the planet.** They're breeding like rabbits; it's over. Need to get rid of some people." And he just totally *meant* it. You could see that **his vision was so dark—he saw a planet covered with subhumans that are just multiplying like maggots** and ruining the planet—and he *did* call them a virus: human life was a virus that he said was destined to spread to other planets. And he's right.

And now you can see that the major powerful people on the planet support this vision of terraforming Mars. Because **all the world leaders and big corporate heads realize that two or three generations from now, they've gotta have an *escape place*.**

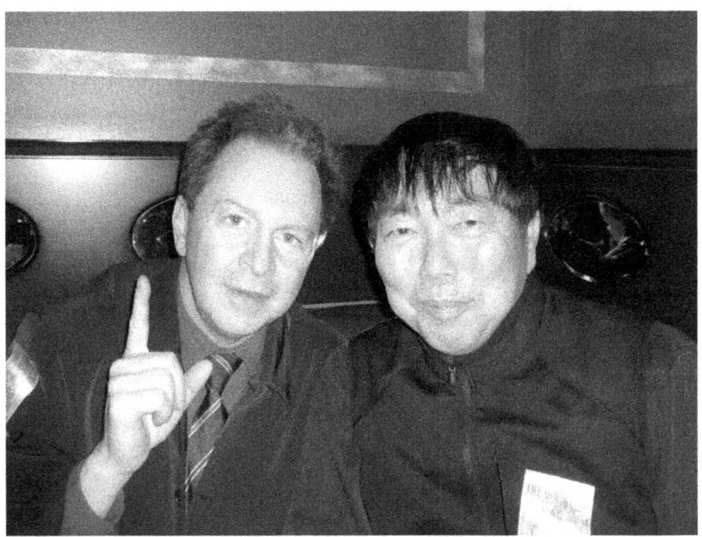

Gerald V. Casale and V. Vale

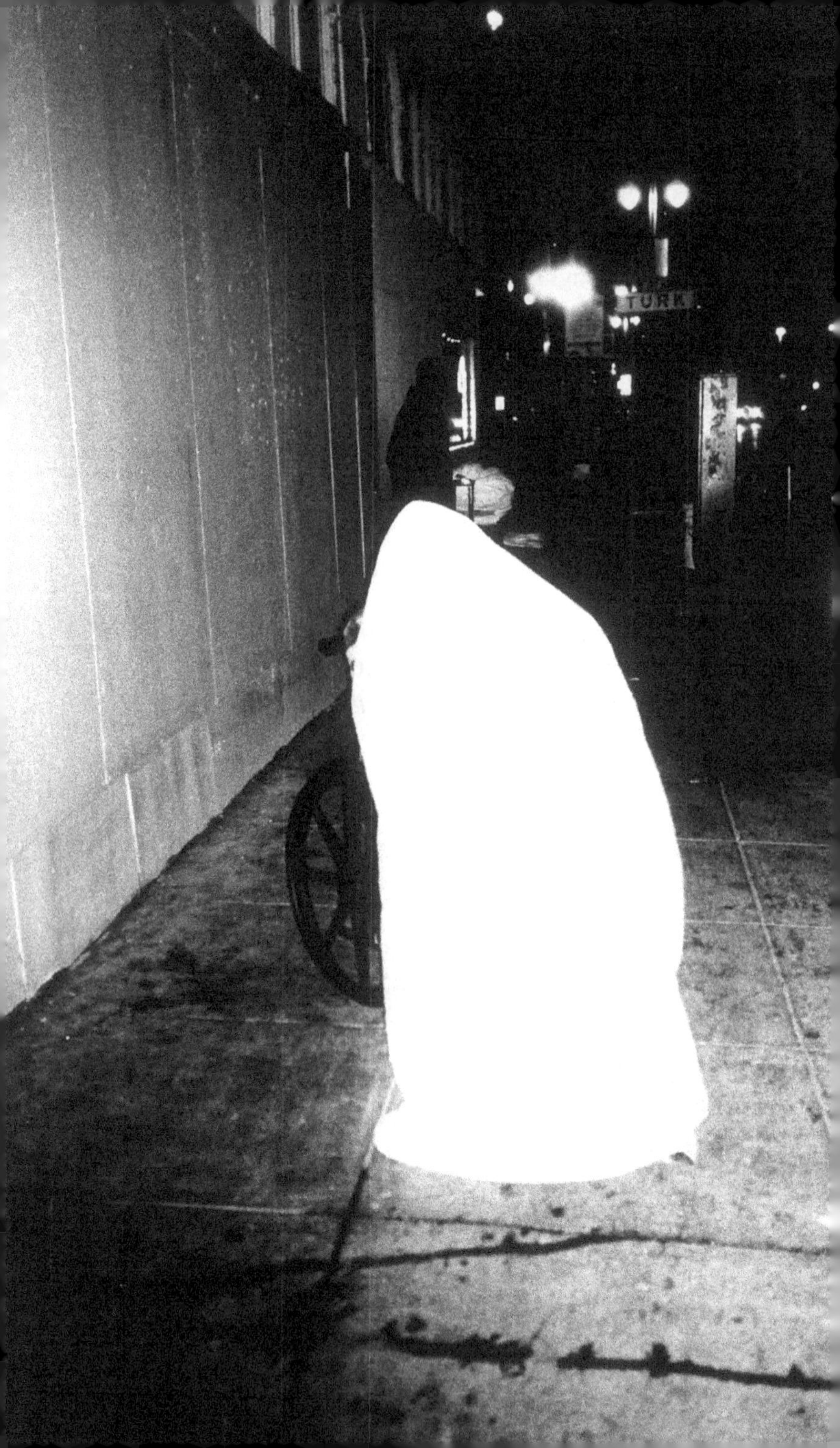
TURK

BRION GYSIN:
The Disaster Tapes

Artist and writer Brion Gysin [January 19, 1916-July 13, 1986] was a long-time friend and collaborator of William S. Burroughs—who described Gysin as "the only man I ever respected." V. Vale and Gysin collaborated on two projects which were fraught with complications and never completed. Vale taped Gysin on several occasions; the tapes presented here were recorded at his Paris apartment in 1985. Vale never succeeded in getting a lengthy interview without being interrupted—that's part of the reason for the title, The Disaster Tapes. *Various humans dropped by and left, blithely interrupting whatever conversation might have been trying to be born. Vale was hoping to get hard facts about the Surrealists, but Gysin was an uncompromising gossip whose penchant for scandal is dangerously extreme (and may even be untruthful; a word to the wise). Nevertheless, he was a fascinating storyteller. We hope Gysin fans can glean glimmers of inspiration from the following transcripts, which are published here for the first time.*

1. AN INTERVIEW WITH BRION GYSIN (February 27, 1985)

Vale: First of all you had to meet somebody, right?

Photo: Yoshi Yubai

Brion Gysin: I met a dog. A delightful dog came up to me on the terrace of the dome in Montparnasse: a boxer. We immediately became great friends. He belonged to somebody that I'd seen around and thought, "Well, that's someone to avoid," but when he turned out to be the owner of the dog we got to know each other. He was an American Jew from Boston whose family had owned theaters, and he had been brought up in the world of the Barrymores and the other great theatrical families. He had taken a degree to become a medical doctor, gone to Berlin to take his doctorate, and then gotten himself into all sorts of kinky troubles in the late thirties. I guess I must have met him in '37, I should think; maybe '38. I was just back from some hideous misadventures in Greece, and he said that he was going down to spend the spring in the Pyrenees, and why didn't I come along with him and the dog? He had been there several times already on a mysterious search, which little by little he began talking to me about.

He was a larger-than-life character, both physically and in every other way. He'd been previously on the trail of the Cathars, who'd been slaughtered while walled up in the caves in the Pyrenees. Lots of them had been burnt alive; others had been walled up or thrown over cliffs. Their story is very complex, really, and not as simple as all that. He had a rather flimsy story of having been persecuted in Germany. He was pretty good at being persecuted; wherever he went he managed to get persecuted, as I remember.

I had nothing else to do, and since the dog and I were such great friends I went with them to a place called Ussat-les-Bains. It had been a spa in the mid-nineteenth century, very near to Foix and the passage into Andorra—a tiny principality in the Pyrenees. The latter belongs half to the Spanish Bishop of Urgell and half to the President of France, and is a sort of smuggler's paradise. It must be very well run since it never gets into the newspapers. The American had had a group of strange friends who had been there previously with him, and they had done preliminary explorations of these Cathar caves. He knew the local authorities, like the schoolmaster who had spent his whole life going through the caves himself and knew a great deal about the history of the Cathars.

He thought there was this menacing "power" somewhere shifty, which he said was an emissary of Alfred Rosenberg, the Nazi who was the head of Hitler's commission to start a new religion—a Hitlerian religion, which nearly got off the ground as a matter of fact. But he needed three things. The first was the Spear of Longinus, which he got from the Austrians.

V: It's now in a museum in Vienna, isn't it?

BG: That's right. Supposedly it was one of the reasons for Hitler's invasion of Austria. He also needed the Iron Crown of Hungary, which was supposed to have been made out of several nails from the "true cross." And then the Holy Grail, and then he'd be—

V: Master of the World.

BG: Master of the World. I found after a short time that I really didn't like caves.

V: Well, now you've arrived at these caves—just you and this doctor—

BG: That's right, and the dog. We stayed at this hotel which was crumbling apart. We were the only two guests at this hotel. It was run by a woman who had inherited it, and who did the cooking and had a child or two, and her husband, who had been a no-good sailor of some kind. Nat Wolfe, Doctor Wolfe, the [American] cat's name, started in making his own absinthe; he had a great recipe for making absinthe. So he started up all these alembics—

V: Isn't absinthe supposed to have an alchemical origin?

BG: Right. He had *the* alchemical recipe for making absinthe, which was a knockout, I must say.

He went off someplace and left me alone there. He came back a total disaster, having been set upon, robbed, and tattooed with a razor by some people into whose hands he'd fallen in Marseilles. They tattooed a big pig on his fat chest!

V: While he was asleep?

BG: Yes.

V: Do you suppose it was because he'd gotten too drunk on his own absinthe, and passed out?

BG: Too many people in one bed is always a mistake! Obviously, the pig had to be *redesigned,* and the patron's husband, the ex-sailor, said that he knew how to do tattooing if we could only get some very fine embroidery needles—three you needed; you tie them all together. I said that this pig could be turned into the head of a bull, using the pig's back as the broad forehead of the bull. His curly tail was a bit of a problem, but it could become one crumpled horn and one upright horn. [laughs] So I spent the evenings tattooing my friend.

V: *You* did? Not the sailor?

BG: No, the ex-sailor showed me how, and then I did it.

V: Did you use regular India ink?

BG: Yeah. I started begging off these underground expeditions saying that I had claustrophobia. Every day they went out, and in the evenings we sat around drinking his absinthe and tattooing—free tattooing. God, I took some beautiful photographs of that, but they got lost.

V: So you've been a tattoo artist as well? And a welder, too. You explored these caves, but you didn't really find anything satisfactory?

BG: Oh yeah. We came across places where people had been walled up, and breaking through the wall we found a lot of skeletons which been there for a long, long, long, long time.

V: So you actually broke through the wall with pickaxes? No wonder you didn't like it; that's a lot of work!

BG: I didn't like it, being in the caves.

V: Did you feel it was dangerous?

BG: No, I just got claustrophobia until I couldn't stand

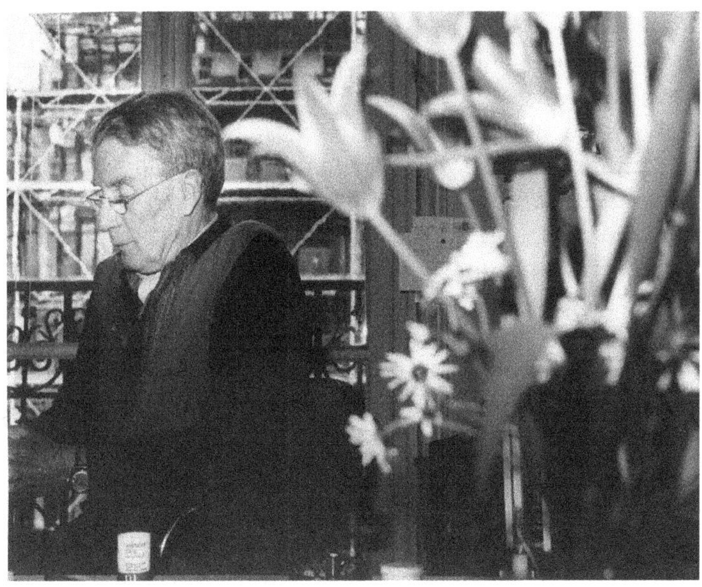

Brion Gysin, Paris

it any longer. The local schoolteacher was half a friend but a little bit jealous of "the rich folk from Paris who were coming down and trampling on his territory." He had found remarkable things there, like a few Egyptian amulets of turquoise-blue baked clay. That seemed to prove that these caves had been known for a long time, and had been *rue du passage* from anywhere in the Mediterranean that you'd like to name, like Tel Aviv or Jerusalem or wherever, to Marseilles, which was a Greek colony originally.

One of the most famous books of the discovery of the ancient world was written by somebody from Marseilles; I've forgotten his name—whiskey clouds my memory! It's about the first voyage to England, to the Tin Islands, by some Greek fink who stowed away on a Carthaginian ship. You know, the Greeks and the Carthaginians and the alphabet and everything are all mixed up and the relationships are still not solved. The story of Cadmus and the alphabet is presumably of Phoenician origin…

Anyhow, people from Egyptian times had passed through there on their way to the Tin Islands—Cornwall, west of England. And the Grail was supposed to have been taken, after the Last Supper, by Joseph of Arimathea and Mary Magdalene who had set up in business together and took off for the Tin Islands to save themselves from the Roman persecution. They had gone to Glastonbury, where Joseph had planted a thorn tree which still blossoms in Glastonbury to this very day, according to the hippies. Then he'd made his way back to that area in the Pyrenees and had left the Grail with the people who later became the Cathars. Centuries later, King Arthur did the Round Table with Perceval, Gawain and the boys—they were all super-excited by the Grail legend.

There was a particular cave entrance that had a smallish platform about the size of this room, maybe nine by twelve feet, which had obviously been built up with a wall to make a flat platform. The entrance to the cave was straight ahead, and the platform stood to the left of the cave entrance. In an abutment of rock that came up there was a cave with not just an entrance, but also a window looking right down over the valley, so you could see who was coming up the road—if it was Simon de Montfort with his Cathar-killers.

I spent quite some time here looking while the others explored. While lying on the ground smoking, I noticed mason's marks up on the ceiling, which meant that the cave was an artificial one: somebody had cut the whole ceiling and dropped it. If you do a job like that, it's obviously because you have something to hide. And if there was a hiding place, like in the Edgar Allan Poe story "The Purloined Letter," you don't hide it at the bottom of the cave but at the *door,* where no one would think to look. Just then Hitler's envoy—the Rosenberg man—in Paris began to move the local authorities to ask us about our papers. It was time to leave.

I've never been back. Nat Wolfe went on to all sorts of adventures in other countries; he was a bullfight critic in Mexico and a child psychologist in New York. He was very much a Wandering Jew.

V: One thing I'd like to find out, Brion, is how you intersected with the "Beats." You mentioned Gregory Corso, and I didn't even know that you knew him. Where was it? New York?

BG: No, Paris.

V: Really? When? I know that some of them, like Ferlinghetti for instance, were here in World War II and simply stayed on in Paris in the forties. My uncle was here, too.

BG: And stayed?

V: No, but he lived here for a while a painter. He knew Ferlinghetti and a lot of the "Beats" from those days, although not too well. So were you in Paris in '49? Is that where you met Corso?

BG: Eek. Well, I met Burroughs in Tangiers in '53, and then found him again in Paris in '58. I was having an exhibition of very small desert paintings, which either have to be miniature or as big as the desert. I was showing a notebook that I had made on a trip through the desert in the winter of '51–'52. So I was having the show in '53 when Burroughs came in after a trip through Mexico and the Amazon. (I've written about that in various places.) I saw very little of him during all of that time, which was when he was writing those long letters to Allen Ginsberg. [Mohamed] Hamri and I opened 1001 Nights [a restaurant] there toward the end of '53, and Burroughs used to come there once a month on payday with Alan Ansen. But I hardly knew him; he kept his distance, spoke only Spanish, and couldn't mix. There were so many Spaniards there that you couldn't frequent both Spaniards and Moroccans, as they were like oil and water.

I saw him again, after I had lost the restaurant and had gone on to a circuit of shows in New York, Rome, London, and finally here in Paris. I ran into Burroughs in the Place Saint-Michel, while he was living in the Beat Hotel. I went there to see him, and eventually moved in myself—that's when Gregory [Corso] showed up. He was very attractive and very troublesome.

V: Yeah, he'd been in jail in America. He was like a Greek Punk: wild, yet he could write, too. A real contradiction.

BG: He can be very difficult to this day.

V: I see him all the time in San Francisco. Last time

I saw him he accused me of ignoring him! I didn't realize he knew or even recognized me. I had worked at City Lights and saw him, but we had never *talked* or anything.

BG: He had already broken in the window and taken the cash box?

V: Yeah. I was working there when that happened. I kind of admired him for that—even Ferlinghetti sort of did, I think. It's funny; he does that, and then the next day he's out of the country to Italy... I met Alan Ansen once, but he seemed sad and quiet.

BG: When was that?

V: When I was a kid.

BG: I find him a little creepy, actually. We're not recording that, I hope... [laughs] Use "strange"—

V: Well, I just didn't understand him. He seemed like he was off in his own world—very incommunicative. He was trying to paint; he had several paintings with him, and I thought, "God, they're bad."

[laughter]

BG: Apparently he's very learned.

V: You collaborated with Sinclair Beiles. Who is he, and where did he come from?

BG: He comes from a South African Jewish family. His mother had owned a pharmacy or something like that. She may still, and he may be back there. He flipped out a couple of times.

V: Violent?

BG: Yeah. He played an important role very briefly. He was employed by Maurice Girodias, for whom he had written an erotic book whose title I can't remember. It was an adaptation or steal from some Chinese classic [*Houses of Joy*, published by Olympia Press in 1958 under the pseudonym Wu Wu Meng]. He worked as a liaison between Girodias and Burroughs over the *Naked Lunch* manuscript, bringing daily proofs from the printers and all that. He was quite an attractive character when he was younger and saner.

V: Very well-read, at that point?

BG: Yes, he was. He played quite a role in William's life; he had an income—which he shared with him! He moved into the Beat Hotel and proceeded to flip out. He was all right, in his own funny way.

V: You haven't seen him in a long time?

BG: I saw him once. I very rarely turn people away at the door, but I saw him once so strange, so physically changed and menacing, that I said, "I'm sorry, but I'm terribly busy and cannot see you."

V: That was polite. Especially if he looked menacing... Did you know Tobias Schneebaum [author of *Keep the River on Your Right*]?

BG: Yeah, we had a lot of things in common. Some horrible things in common, actually—he also had a colostomy.

V: Oh, really? How old is he, by the way?

BG: I don't know. He'd been converted to Catholicism by

Dorothy Day and her Neo-Catholic business. Then he got really into the chains-and-leather scene, all the leather bars, and discovered that that was where his *real* tastes lay. He decided he would like to meet some cannibals because he had heard about "cannibalistic homosexuality"—

V: What in the world is that?

BG: They keep their women completely apart, never eating them because they think that it is "bad meat." He went to the Amazon by way of Peru—

V: So the homosexuality refers only to the meat-eating?

BG: No, no… The whole lifestyle and ritual. He went to Peru to attempt to "enter" some of this, and he met some young intellectuals in Lima, including this one friend who was (as many Spanish intellectuals are) prone to saying, "*I'm thinking... I'm thinking... I'm thinking about going to the Amazon someday,*" but never actually *going* there!

So Tobias said he would send letters to a Catholic priest who had established a mission at the head of the Amazon, ensuring that they would *really* get there. When they arrived, they discovered a very strange set-up—the one very amusingly described in his book. He felt he was wasting his time there, and so after asking the Padre how to get to cannibal country, he was told to "keep the river on his right."

So he is walking through the jungle, with a high canopy over his head, when suddenly from among the tree trunks there appear a number of highly decorative-looking cannibals. He quickly takes off all of his clothes, gets an erection, and begins to touch their penises. They are immediately delighted by this and ask him home, so he goes to back to their village and finds out how their community works and *whatnot.* They go on one hunt without him, after which, since he has picked up a boyfriend and enough of the lingo to make himself understood, he tells them that the next time they go on a hunt, he would like to go along.

Meanwhile Schneebaum's friend, whose name was Alfonso or Luis, finally has gotten up enough courage—

V: The Spanish-speaking intellectual that he'd met?

BG: Yes. He's traveling in one direction, and Tobias and the cannibals in the other, and it turns out that he is whom they *get*. So he eats his friend. He's always been a little vague about it! He got back and published his book with some success.

V: I find that a little hard to believe...

BG: That it had success?

V: No, that story.

BG: Well, at the same time as that, [supposedly] Michael Rockefeller went down there with all his video equipment and offered to pay them [the cannibals] to kill and eat each other. They took his video camera, smashed it over his head, and ate *him.* Schneebaum was contacted by Nelson Rockefeller, who offered to invite him to the "sea island plantation-shack for indigent writers" [laughter] on the condition that he look for and eat the people who had eaten Michael. I've never been able to find out what happened, as he is a bit skittish. I've heard about it from Burroughs, who'd been out there staying with them, and I wrote back and asked him to find out what happened.

Who ate who is still a little bit up in the air. William was a little vague about it, and he never answered that part of the letter...

Paul Bowles has been sick for over forty years.

V: Paul Bowles? From what?

BG: From living in Mexico.

V: Not from Tangiers?

BG: What has he had that you shouldn't have? He's a whole poem, him and his health. Typhoid he's had, in Tangiers.

V: Typhoid? I thought they'd wiped that out.

BG: He's had typhoid a couple of times. When we lived together, we took all sorts of precautions, except that while we shared the house together we also shared expenses, so lots of incidents occurred like, "I haven't drunk very much wine so you'd better pay for it," and, "You ate half of that tomato."

V: Christ!

BG: It got pretty bad. During that time, we insisted on each paying for half of the pills to put in the water (so as not to get sick). If you were told not to do something because you'd get worms—and you did it—you'd get sick. You had to take this medicine which made your shit purple, and the worms would itch your ass so bad that you'd hardly be able to sit still in your chair.

V: Who'd want to live like that?

BG: I've never had them since. In all the twenty-two years that I lived in Tangiers, I never had them again and I never took another precaution. It was only when I *was* taking precautions that I got sick!

I remember washing oranges, and that really staggered me. When washing salad you had to put in potassium permanganate, which dyed the water wine color, and you had to wash every leaf. I never did *that* again, either! They always said that that was where the worms were coming from. "You just don't know, Brion," they used to tell me.

V: Did you ever meet Philip Lamantia? He went to Tangiers.

BG: Oh yeah. He went to jail there, too.

V: Yeah, I know; for a week. Paul got him out.

BG: Did he?

V: Yeah. Paul intervened and talked to someone he knew to let him out.

BG: He's a wimp. Don't you think he's a real wimp?

V: I don't know. I don't look at him that way. Did you ever talk to him?

BG: Oh yeah.

V: You must have been pretty young, then.

BG: Yeah, we all were.

Anonymous Guest: How does your wine glass go down while I never see you take a sip?

BG: It's all part of the technique. [laughter] You never see a real drinker taking a drink; I heard this about someone else recently and had to laugh. It's quite true. With a real drinker, you have to watch the level of the wine against the label on the *bottle,* not the glass. ◆◆

2. THE DISASTER TAPE (February 27, 1985)

In this recording, several men talk who are unidentified. We call them: X, Y and Z.

BG: J. Paul Getty hasn't done anything since the museum was built. He's dead, no?

V: Brion, can you backtrack a second: J. Paul Getty has always been fascinated by the Beats?

BG: So he [the protagonist of Gysin's novel *The Last Museum*, partially based on J. Paul Getty] wants to buy the hotel, and he gets there to buy it, and he doesn't realize that it's turned into the Bardo: because it's seven floors, seven rooms on each floor; it has forty-nine rooms in it, like that. He's told that he has to move into Room One. That's the way it starts off (in Room One) and then he moves up the different floors. Each floor is different—well, it's a Tibetan book: highly rewritten, and very funny—hilariously, horrendously funny.

V: 'Cuz he has to go through all the soul's successive stages—

BG: We only follow him up to the fifth floor where he falls into a *womb trap* which this girl has always been warning him against—I mean, *several* times he falls into some traps like this. But it's all a sort of *roman a clef* as well—some people are quite *recognizable*. I told all of this to Paul Getty, telling him—trying to be *sure* he wouldn't object. He was very amused by what he heard, but I don't know whether I'll send him *this* version until later perhaps. 'Cuz he and I were great friends until the death of Talitha [the wife who died of a heroin overdose in 1971] and *whatnot.* Then his son, little Paul [John Paul Getty III], who lost the ear [Getty III was famously kidnapped and had his ear cut off and sent to a newspaper], was also a *very* close friend of mine until he crashed into a vegetable state and everything. He's paralyzed and blind. Not deaf, but he's blind and can't speak and can't move. He's with Gail, his mother, in Brentwood.

X: Who paid for his hospital?

BG: It was at home. Me, I was very angry about all these things. Little Paul used to come here, and he'd say, "*You* phone daddy so I can talk to him." So I'd phone Paul and say, "Oh, by the way, little Paul is here, and he'd like to speak to you" and I'd pass him the telephone: "Daddy, it's little Paul." Then he had this hideous accident from being left unconscious for too long, so he had irreparable brain damage from 72 hours in a coma. And when they got him out of the coma—'cuz they'd thought, "Oh, yeah he's *always* passing out—yeah yeah, he's upstairs there." Nobody looked after him at all.

X: Was it drugs?

BG: There was a mixture—yeah, there were drugs there, of course. But it was sorta wrong. I've known him ever since he was a little kid. And we liked each other a lot and I liked his father less and less because of all this.

X: He seemed not to have cared when little Paul was kidnapped.

BG: Well, they thought it was a *gag.* They thought that he'd just done it to get some money out of him. He has no money at all; no money coming to him because he broke the rules of Sarah C. Getty's will, which was written because she thought that J. Paul Getty would be a no-good and would never make any money. So she wrote one of the greatest watertight wills in history. It says, among other things, that no heir can marry before the age of 25. Little Paul, because his mother and father were divorced (and Gail didn't know anything about that; she'd never even *read* the will or really even knew about it, even)… he went and married one of these German chicks, these twins who were models in Rome in those days. He married Gisela Martine Getty, so there was no money for him AT ALL. Nor will there ever be.

The whole story of their money and vast fortune and everything else is very torturous. J. Paul is in the hospital all the time now—and for some years. So I went to see

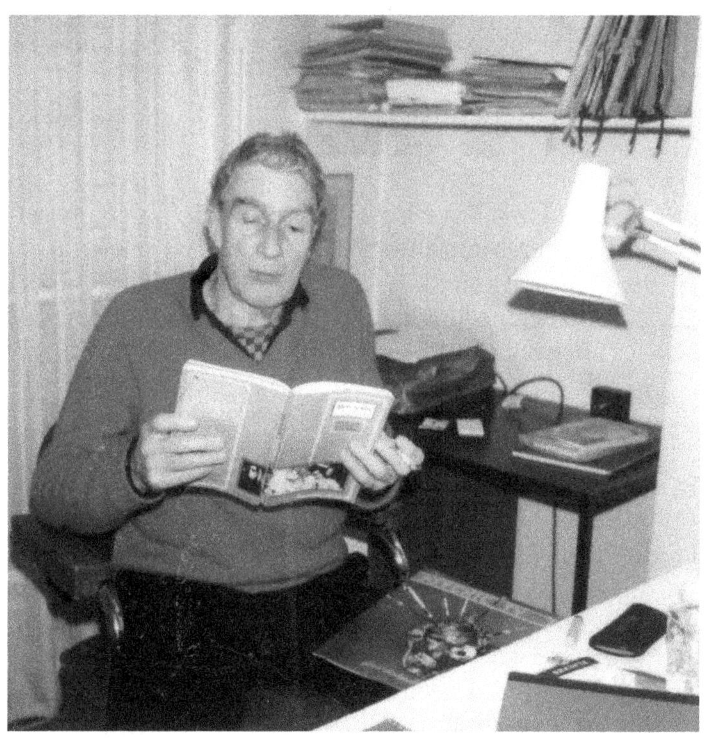

Brion Gysin, Paris

him at the hospital when I was over there in November.

V: Where, in November?

BG: In London. He was *very*, very touched that I was sort of making up for this coolness between us. And he's been giving money away, rather unexpectedly. He gave the British government £450,000 in order to pay for that picture that they thought they were going to lose... what I call the "Dubious Duccio". [In 1984 J. Paul Getty contributed £750,000 to a £1.8m fund to keep a Crucifixion by Duccio in the U.K.] I mean art history isn't even quite certain that Duccio ever really *existed* even, but there was this picture being bought by the Getty Museum. He's on bad terms with the Getty Museum and with his brother Gordon, who's now the richest man in the world.

X: Is Gordon in San Francisco?

BG: L.A. and San Francisco. He's a musician, a composer. He writes operas and things like that.

[The group begins looking at Gysin's scrapbook of recent articles about himself.]

X: What were *those* photos used for?

BG: Rock magazines—supposedly for my rock record. My rock record's gone nowhere—it's a hideous tragedy. I didn't even get paid.

X: It's publicity for you.

BG: Do you think I need some of this publicity? Publicity I can't *eat,* I've noticed! If I could eat it, it might change things...

V: When did you meet J. Paul Getty, the one who's in the hospital in London?

BG: I met him when he divorced Gail and married a girl I knew called Talitha.

V: Where?

BG: In Morocco.

V: When was this?

BG: '67.

V: At a party or something?

BG: No, no they came to see *me.* Through friends, they knew I was there. It was a case of love at first sight. They went down to Marrakech, and—you know, the really rich can never, never, never turn down a bargain! So he found this crumbling palace which was in a very bad legal state even. It had belonged to a French man who wasn't allowed to come back to Morocco anymore. So he was able to buy it for *very* little money! And he came back from Marrakech and said, "I just bought this place for *YOU* to live in, Brion!" I said, "I don't like Marrakech—it was *on purpose* that I live here in Tangier." "Yeah, yeah, but you come down there." I said, "Look, I'm not going to come and be your concierge—don't be silly." But, I did go down for a *while*. We had all sorts of strange adventures, particularly with the royal family. All the king's sisters, all those princesses were naturally *wildly intrigued* and couldn't be kept out of the house!

V: The King of Morocco, you mean?

BG: Yeah. He was telling 'em, "Be careful—there's *drugs*

in the house, don't take any drugs there." I thought it was time to leave, and I did. And then Talitha died of an overdose, and that kind of cooled our friendship. But then I became such good friends with little Paul who was in a terrible mess, after having his ear cut off and all that—really it was *horrible*. They sent the ear through the mail, and the mail works so badly in Italy that it took two weeks to get from Naples to Rome. And the old man said, "That isn't an ear. I'm not gonna give any money… no money at all." It took an awful long time to get him freed from the mafia who had sold him. The people who kidnapped him then sold him to some other people who were the ones who cut off his ear…

So… naturally it almost gave me the idea to write a hilariously funny book about death [*The Last Museum*]. Also a hilariously funny book about feminists—and lesbians, and those things. 'Cuz each floor has a different crew of impossible people living on it. It's funny, it's very very funny, I think. Roll around on the floor in stitches of laughter.

Y: There's a story of you buying a Max Ernst—is that a secret?

BG: Oh yes. [quickly changes topic] I must look for the Keith Haring book because you have to see that. The new one. Have you seen the *Manipulator?* I've got texts in all of those. Beautiful photograph of—

Y: Who has been arrested for graffiti?

BG: Keith Haring. For drawing in the subway. You see what I mean about "bled up to the edges"? And it should be a book which is an *object*. Not a book to *read*; not a book to pontificate over… The sun sets at six o'clock. I never drink before the sun sets.

V: You and J.G. Ballard. He sends his best to you by the way.

BG: You saw him?

V: Just two days ago.

BG: He told you that I was at his luncheon for getting the prize from *The Guardian*?

V: Yeah, he said he was glad to meet you. We'd given him a copy of *Here To Go*, so he was aware of you.

BG: That lunch was *something else.* I'd never been; I'd *heard* about such things as a "British literary lunch." [whistles] That was something else—I mean: a parade of monsters. Ooh; eek! Something else; high-powered stuff. The whole British *disestablished establishment* was there. I see he didn't get the big prize, the Booker Prize.

V: Because so many people had predicted in the media that he would.

BG: That's why he didn't get it. Just like poor Graham Greene never got the Nobel Prize because everybody said he was going to get it. So they wouldn't give it to him. Just meanness, I think.

V: They have to prove how "independent" in judgment they are.

BG: I will never write another book, maybe not even another letter!

V: Backtrack for me, back to the first floor—

BG: Well, the first floor is naturally the hardest. There

are three famous cases in history. [Thomas] Carlyle lost the manuscript—the maid threw the manuscript of *The French Revolution* into the fire, so he had to sit down and write it again. T.E. Lawrence lost *The Seven Pillars of Wisdom*—he left it in London in Waterloo Station in a place where you leave your luggage, and it was never seen again. So he had to sit down and write *that* again.

V: What's the third?

BG: It was Malcolm Lowry who lost *Under the Volcano* [actually *Ultramarine*]... misplaced, stolen... [laughs] But since Xerox and photocopy it's not so dangerous anymore. It took those girls only an hour to turn me out those seven manuscripts... But, as I say I started writing this in 1968, so how long ago was that? More years than I like to think. [17 years]

As soon as I'd finished *The Process* I got a contract—an *advance*—of $5,000 from Doubleday. And so I sat down and thought, "Well, I'll just write *anywhere*; start a book." And it wasn't so easy to do. Still, they *refused* that. So I was *free* from the Doubleday contract, but I hadn't really advanced at all. That was I don't know how many manuscripts ago—since then, maybe ten different manuscripts. And the whole thing got more solid and got its self organized over this long, long period. I think that now it goes like a whiz, practically.

William phoned me up [about *Cities of the Red Night*]. I had gone through the manuscript several times and changed the end. There's a piece which wasn't the end, which is now the end. He said, "Yes, Brion, what you got to do is, you gotta be careful about the *narrative flow.*" I said, "Wait a minute, you heard that from some cheap agent—some cheap Madison Avenue agent, didn't you?"

[Gap in conversation] ...D'Annunzio was writing a long play about Saint Sebastian, so he got himself a bow and arrow and started shooting at the servants. You can't do that anymore. You're not allowed to do that since the Second World War—the *First* World War!

V: Wait, this is Gabriele D'Annunzio?

BG: Yeah.

V: I just saw a biography of him by Philippe Jullian. Is that worth reading?

BG: Philippe Jullian, eh? Really? He was a very *mondaine* artist who drew caricatures of fashionable people and wrote gossip notes and things. Yeah. I guess that would be absolutely down his alley. Is that an interesting book? Is it valuable? A valid book?

V: I just saw it in a store in London a couple days ago.

BG: I knew Philippe Jullian!

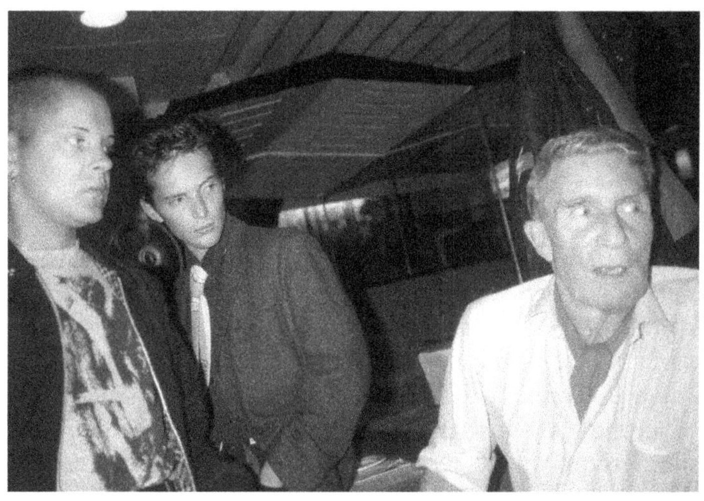

Genesis P-Orridge, Ramuntcho Matta and Gysin at the Final Academy, 1982

V: Where? Here?

BG: Yeah yeah, he was always everywhere. Every cocktail party, every tea party… There is a very charming lady, whose invitation I had meant to accept, but I got the number of her house wrong, so I arrived at 421 instead of 221 or something like that… When I couldn't find her number anywhere, I looked in the telephone book first of all, and I thought, "Oh, Goddamn these people." You have to pay extra money *not* to be in the telephone book.

V: Yeah, same in America.

Y: Ten bucks in Europe.

BG: Well I don't know why they do at all—it's so mean!

Y: Why so cheap? [laughter]

BG: Why so cheap?! Why not make them pay a *thousand* dollars to stay out of trouble? I thought, "Well then, *where* would I find a social register?" So I went to my friend Anna Bavaria and said, "You must have the—" "Of course, dear!"

Y: [later] I would like very much to go to Egypt.

BG: Yeah, I've been only once. I went on a great adventure during a time that I was utterly fucking penniless in the Beat Hotel—I mean not one cent! I don't mean little money, just no money at all. Burroughs had no money, I had no money, and suddenly: I had shown my Dream Machine at a show in 1962 called "L'Object," which is in the Louvre Museeé des Arts Decoratifs. And people from Philips, the people who make electric light bulbs and radios and all that kind of thing, had been interested in anything that was electrical or moving, and they were particularly interested in a sculptor called [Nicolas] Schöffer, whom they had backed with lots and lots of money—I mean hundreds of thousands of dollars. And right next to his big display they saw my Dream Machine. So we started talking and then they started coming 'round, but when they found me living in such *really* miserable conditions as the Beat Hotel they went, "Eww…" [laughter]

So I said to them once, "How did you meet Nicolas Schöffer?" And they said, "Well, that was *very* difficult." And I said, "What do you mean?" They said, "Well, we were told that if we came to Paris and stayed in the *best* hotel, he would send a messenger around who would tell us how to find him. So we stayed one day and we stayed two days and we stayed three days and no messenger appeared, so we were getting ready to leave and his messenger arrived and said, 'There will be cars for you tonight at midnight.'"

This was in the days of those black Citroen taxis that really looked like gangster films, and *two* of them were in front of the hotel. And these stiff rich Dutch industrialists went down and got into them—shady-looking characters at the wheel. They went 'round and 'round zig-zag for hours, up streets and down alleys 'til they didn't know *which* part of Paris they were in, or anything. Finally, they *screech* to a stop in an impasse—a *cul-de-sac* where you couldn't go any further—and they were ordered to "Get out."

So they got out; it was completely dark. Suddenly they realized there was *another* cul-de-sac—another ten meters or so to go. Then a door *slowly* opened. And inside everything was buzzing! Electrical things were twinkling and moving and swirling all over the place. A man with white hair, dressed entirely in white wearing a long white scientist's smock, was… Nicolas Schöffer. So they put *all* of their money on it, right away.

V: Jeez, just for the show, huh?

BG: The show. I thought, "This is *it!*" [laughter] So they came to the Beat Hotel and one of them slipped on some *shit* on the staircase [laughter] and put his back out. And I realized then—

V: Your show wasn't "up to snuff"—

BG: I was just not up to snuff *like that.* I've had several other terrible mishaps, like with famous collectors... like the Briton Tremaines from Connecticut [sic] who would come and say [British accent], "Well, *this* hasn't been painted by a *really great* artist like De Kooning." So obviously I was working the wrong side of the tracks!

Z: This would be the perfect text: all the disasters—

BG: —disaster text: what a long series of them! Pretty funny, too. Because one day I said to the people, "What are you doing?" And they said, "Well, you know we have so much money and our friend's doing so well that we decided we wanted to do something to help artists. So we've commissioned Schöffer to do a—". And he had done a big wall beside a canal in Holland or Northern Belgium—I've forgotten where it was—which is very effective, when photographed at night particularly, with the lights blinking and twinkling and turning a little bit and the whole thing reflected in water... they had laid out a lot of money for that.

Then they offered him a thing that has never come true—*his* life is full of frustrations, too! He was supposed to do that whole new section of Paris out there at the end of the avenues, where you have the perspective that goes into La Défense (as it's called), which is a jumble of different-shaped skyscrapers that were all supposed to be symmetrical. He was to have a tower at the end which was gonna tell the weather and forecast the future for all of them. He says it never came about in *his* life, either.

One day they phoned up, which was very difficult to do because the telephone was downstairs in the bistro, and Madame Rachou would go out in the street and yell, "Monsieur Brion!" I go answer the phone and they said, "Would you like to come around to the office? We have something to tell you." I thought, "How am I going to get there?" I didn't even have money for a metro ticket, and it was way off in the tenth *arrondissement.*

So I walked and I walked and I walked and I finally got there sweaty and tired, and they said, "You speak Arabic, don't you?" And I said, "Well, yeah, I speak Moroccan Arabic." "Well you see, we're in *trouble.* We have one man that's gone to Machu Picchu to put up the sound and light spectacle there. Somebody else is doing the sound and light for the Liberty Bell in Philadelphia, somebody else is doing the Red Fort of Agra in India… All these different things are going on, and we have nobody to send to *Egypt.*

"And we have a problem because Nasser came to our sound and light spectacle at the pyramids"—which is really brilliant, the only spectacle I've ever *seen* in fact, and it's superb. The Sphinx, you sit just a few yards in front of the Sphinx and the Sphinx lights up and begins to *talk* and tells you four thousand years of history in any language; choose a night and you can get the language that you want to hear…

There was a really mad French Copt, and he had this special paper made and a reproduction of Champollion's notes about the discovery of—a facsimile of the notes and pages [possibly *Principes généraux de l'écriture sacrée*, facsimile edition published 1984] and it's a book about *that* thick.

I saw this article written about it, and I immediately wrote to the man and said, "I want a copy of it sent to William Burroughs for his birthday." And it got to him! And William was just [whistles] right out of his mind, 'cuz he's been into that long before *I* ever knew him—when he was at Harvard in his twenties, he was interested in the hieroglyphs. He said, "I got a book *for the rest of my life.*"

Y: And it's a huge, beautiful book—a facsimile of the *Notebooks of Champollion* [Greek, Coptic, Egyptian, to help to understand the hieroglyphs].

BG: So William got it in time for his birthday.

V: Oh, just recently?

BG: Yeah, February 5th. He wrote me a letter… Do you want me to go ahead and tell you the rest of the story about Egypt?

V: Yeah, about Egypt—yes!

BG: Nasser saw this show at the Sphinx and the pyramids, and he was *so* swept away by it that he said, "I want you to do the same thing for me at the citadel in Cairo. And this is to be this great celebration, the tenth year of my revolution, and I want it to be the whole history of everything that ever happened in the citadel leading up to my ascension to power."

They started this fucking thing, and they couldn't get it off the *ground*. Richard Burton was reading the text in English. I've forgotten who was reading the text in French and Italian and whatever the hell, but they couldn't get the *Arab* version down. They said, "Would you go down and get this off the ground? All it will mean is that you go down there, make a tape and take the next airplane back."

I said, "Mmmm, how much are you going to *pay* me?" They mentioned a sum which seemed to me *huge* at that time. But it wasn't all that much in fact, the way things turned out. You had to go to the Indian Embassy to get a visa into Egypt because at that moment everyone was turning their backs on Nasser.

I arrived there and thought, "Absolute fucking disorder, pandemonium!" Nobody could make up their mind about whether you set a date like "1965" or you said, "One thousand, nine hundred and sixty-five," which is quite different in Arabic and—even in English it's different. There were problems like that that had held up the whole works and just gummed up the whole thing, so *nothing* had been done—*nothing!* No *recording* had even

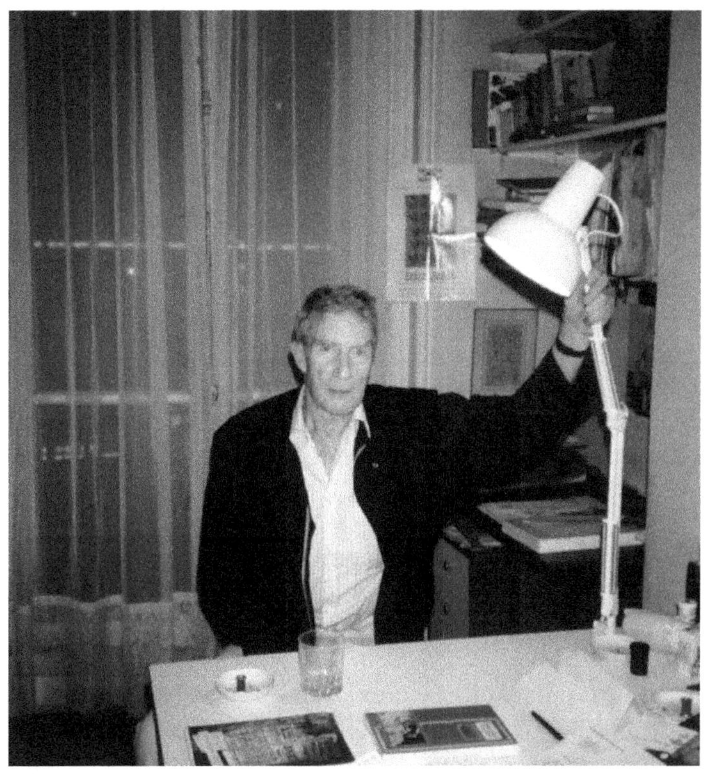

Brion Gysin, Paris

been done at all.

So I was "the engineer from Philips" who went to the Hotel Semiramis instead of going to the one across the street, the new—it was *then* new—the new Chapras. Instead of the new Chapras, they put me up in the Semiramis which is a *dream*. Three weeks later, we had something in the can. But many, many, many an adventure had happened between then and getting this thing in the can which I then brought back.

Z: Wait, you did the Arabic reading?

BG: No, no, I played the English captain. With my accent in Arabic, what else could I do except play a foreigner? So I played the foreigner, and I was the British captain who turned over the citadel to the triumphant forces of the Egyptian revolution, which was a nice thing to do. It was too long an adventure, really, but like most adventures or publicity, you can't *eat* it. But yeah, quite a few adventures.

I was saying—we *began* by saying that I've never been back to Egypt. I would like to go.

Y: The pyramids of Egypt… Americans said that the pyramids are *molten.*

BG: That's the way things are *still* built... It's not true that down that particular shaft, that at certain times you can see certain stars—not at all.

Y: You don't see any rocks coming out, for example.

BG: They've not found any quarries.

Y: It's not natural. Because "natural" is stratification. And this one is not; it's *molten*. Salt, *natron*—it's also a thing to make preservation of the mummy: mix it with sand. Water from the Nile, water from the Aswan, salt from the desert—

BG: Wooden caissons and then they pour it in and pound it down… Everything that's built right across the desert all the way to Southern Morocco is built that way still.

Y: You are going to make a book about Brion? That's good.

V: Two books; I hope to do one of conversations, and one of paintings. The conversations we can afford to do—we know that will happen. The paintings—we might give it to a Japanese publisher who can afford to print color.

Y: But it's very nice to make two books. One book of conversations, one book of pictures.

BG: We will see what happens!

V: Maybe we should go out to dinner.

BG: You go, and we'll go to ours, I'm afraid—you're into that vegetable stuff—

V: What do you mean? I could eat anywhere.

BG: Veggies leave me cold… You know, that was my doctor on the phone right now and he said, "Those two Canadian doctors that I brought to you on a visit last year, are taking a few last looks at the sun in Hawaii right now." And I said, "Cum spots?" Yeah, cum spots.

Z: AIDS?

BG: Yeah, AIDS. I said *what do you mean?* And they come from Edmonton, Alberta. Yeah, even in Edmonton.

Z: Is it big here?

BG: It's so big here that they don't want to talk about it.

V: In Paris.

BG: I bought a gay magazine because there was a boy I know on the cover of one that's just come out. I hardly read the magazine, but it said that the bathhouses had been closed, but I don't know if that's true or not.

V: They did that in San Francisco?

BG: Yeah, apparently they have.

X: What kind of background are you? Korean? Japan?

V: Japan.

BG: You still speak Japanese?

V: No, I never learned. I wasn't raised by my parents.

BG: I went to Japanese language school for those years of the war.

3. LEGENDS OF BRION GYSIN (March, 1985)

V: You said that Napoleon originated Egyptian studies?

BG: Yes. Champollion had the perspicacity to realize that the Rosetta Stone, which was brought back by Napoleon, was the same message in three different languages. And he had studied Coptic. He then first realized that the Egyptian hieroglyphs were not ideograms like the Chinese are, but were actually a syllabary of vocal sounds. The reason why one can pronounce an ancient Egyptian word is that the Coptic language is still spoken.

The only Egyptians in Egypt are the Copts. All the Arabs and Turks are invaders, and all the black people are the slaves they brought up from the south. The Egyptian population, which is very downtrodden and in great difficulty at the present moment, is Coptic, and they looked just exactly like the people on the walls. Napoleon made it a fashion with clothing and particularly furniture; there is a whole period of not-very-well-made French furniture which is called "Return from Egypt" period, and chairs and tables and desks and houses and everything were done in either Pompeiian style, for those who had been on the Italian campaign, or in Egyptian style for those who had been on the Egyptian campaign.

Fürher Marshal [Gebhard Leberecht von] Blücher defeated Napoleon at Waterloo. Now the English idea of Blücher is he arrived too late to the battle, but just in time to grab the emperor's coach and ride into Paris on it. He got a message from the King of Prussia saying, "You have been granted a palace and the title of Prince." Supposedly he wrote back a telegram: "Thanks, Majesty. Furnished or unfurnished?" When the message came back "Unfurnished," he went to Saint-Cloud and picked up the furniture and family portraits of the Bonapartes and everything else that was left.

So much had been destroyed in the French Revolution that when Napoleon came to power, he started commissioning really big historical paintings featuring a great deal of conspicuous consumption; the whole school of David. Dressing and playing up being an emperor, grabbing the crown away from the Pope who was supposed to crown him and he... crowns *himself*. Napoleon was a big actor, and his furniture followed suit.

I spent some of my teen years in a house that belonged to the Blüchers that still had a great deal of this furniture, so I know a lot about it. In fact, when I was 16 I was too big to get into Napoleon's clothes that had been found in his carriage. We used to go to the beach in Guernsey, with his mess kit that he carried, his chamber-pot so he could take a shit in his carriage, and his dinner service so he could be served food while his horses were galloping or in a battlefield or anything like that. It had fallen into Blücher's hands, so we used to go on picnics with it in the 1930's: '32, '33, '34. I don't know where it all is today. I don't think anyone would dream of taking it on a picnic anymore.

V: Well, they might not even recognize what it is?

BG: Blücher gave a lot of it to France; it belongs to some museum system now. This is getting off into gossip—is that what you want in this interview?

V: [laughs] No, let's let nature take its course. I was wondering how one draws, and what one chooses to draw. I remember I was drawing as a kid and this one adult I met showed me how to draw more realistically and that almost ruined drawing for me.

BG: Oh, really?

V: He showed me how to get the shading and little shadows and stuff and I preferred my own style so I quit drawing. [laughs]

BG: I had my first drawing lesson from Nellie Melba. Did you ever hear of Dame Nellie Melba, the great singer of 19th and earliest 20th century?

V: Yeah, I guess, vaguely.

BG: It's in that little book I've written called *Legends of Brion Gysin*, my baby book with all my baby pictures. We were crossing the Atlantic in 1920 when I was four and I was very interested in fairies and nightingales and beautiful thoughts.

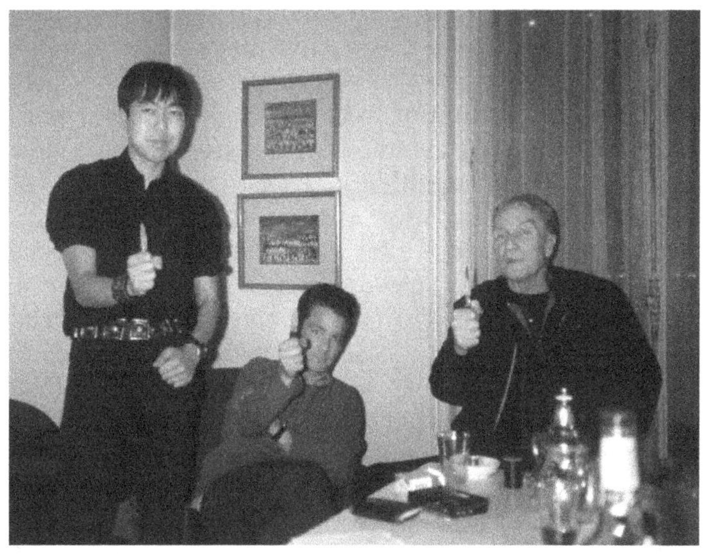

V. Vale (with pen), Bobby Adams and Brion Gysin (with knives), Paris

V: Mythology.

BG: No, no—it was the *beautiful thoughts era* where pregnant ladies had beautiful thoughts for as long as they could (until they started screaming), and children were brought up with nothing but beautiful thoughts around. There was plenty of tragedy with my father having disappeared in the war when I was a few months old, but it was all *smoothed over*. It was all beautiful thoughts and everything.

On the ship going across, I opened the cabin door, and the cabin door across from us was partly open. I heard this divine sound and squeaked to my mother, "Oh, Mommy, listen to the nightingale!" This great big fat lady came out and pulled me to her bosom and said, "The greatest compliment of my entire career! What a marvelous curly-haired child!" It was Melba on her farewell tour, and she found out it was my birthday: January 19, 1920.

She gave me my fourth birthday party, and she drew me a whole lot of drawings. One was a circle, a pond, then there were two trees beside it—scratchy trees. There was a little canal running from the pond to another place where there was a fountain which had a dot in the middle to show the fountain with a spray of water coming out of the side that went into sort of a bird thing, with scratchy trees being long legs of a fat stork or something, and the head being a little bit smaller.

I thought, "So *that's* how you copy the world! You make up a story about the world (or you think you understand a story about the world), and then you illustrate it." So from then on, I was illustrating as I thought it was (or should be). I wasn't encouraged in this at all; nobody saved these things… It was considered impolite to make personal remarks especially to children, so I was never praised for them in any way, or given any recognition—nobody would *think* of putting them up on the wall. (Perhaps in the nursery, servants would put them up on the wall.)

V: Servants? How many did you have?

BG: Oh, other people's servants. Servants had begun to be kind of scarce by that time. I had nannies, of course, who looked after me and gave me their version of the world, ideas of theirs: "This is the man who sells the muffins." In those days in England, there was a man who would ring a bell at four o'clock every afternoon carrying great muffins on a wooden tray on his head: warm crumpets and scones.

Drawing pictures made food come to you; you'd draw pictures about things you'd like to eat and then you'd *get* them to eat! Like a cake or a plum pudding. Yeah, I remember that.

V: It's magic, in a way. So you continued: you never stopped drawing.

BG: I remember then it started to be sex. Food first, and then sex.

V: When, around the age of nine or so?

BG: Something like that. I remember my mother discovered some very small drawings of that kind and she'd face me with them, and in a perfectly reasonable sort of way say, "The only thing I want to know is, is this supposed to be art or is this sex?" And I'd go, "Well, this is art," thinking I might get punished if I said "sex." So I stopped making those kinds of drawings. Maybe I stopped drawing altogether. Sexy drawings were something common children scribbled in public urinals or something. That's what we're right back to, isn't it? Graffiti world.

V: [laughs]

BG: Museums, migod. Museums were very dusty, cold; very poorly attended.

V: But weren't you taken to them when you were young?

BG: Oh, yes. Rich people had *houses* that were museums almost, you know. Lord Blücher's was full of things like that portrait of Napoleon crossing the Alps on a horse. You know, that marvelous picture of the horse rearing up and young Napoleon on his way to Italy. It exists in *three* versions: on a white horse, on a grey horse, and a black horse. They had the grey horse version—a big huge, huge canvas. You'll see it in every history book.

Other people I knew—boys from school—had houses that had inherited works of art. That's essentially what museums were: inherited works of art. There were big museums, the kings' works of art... the kings went out of fashion, and the state let it all gather dust and almost wither away, because it had been the kings' "publicity" and was really of no interest for the new "states."

Museums were dark and dingy and dirty, very poorly lit, not very often open, certainly not places for crowds of people getting in out of the cold and sleeping on the books as they do across the street [at the Beaubourg]. "Absorbing culture," somebody said. "The third world is busy absorbing culture by sleeping on the books."

V: At some point, you had to move into working with a paintbrush. I never reached that stage myself.

BG: I never studied art in school because that was an "extra." At school almost everything was an extra. Tennis was an extra. Art certainly was an extra. Not a terribly good investment, so I never was allowed to take art.

When I was 16 there was a monk at the school who taught art—he'd gone to school for a few years and had kind of a lay life. He'd been interested in painting and come to Paris and studied with Louis Marcoussis. Do you remember who Marcoussis was? He was a Cubist Expressionist or a "classic" Cubist, in the 1920s.

V: No, I'm not familiar with him.

BG: Well, he never quite made it. He had a school and this monk had gone to school there. He taught art. I had a big crush on him; I thought he was infinitely attractive. He was a sculptor himself; that's what he wanted to do. He was a very "gay" character, even though one didn't even know the word in those days…

V: Yeah, and barely the concept.

BG: He allowed me to work in his stone yard when I was 15, 16, 17, 18—something like that.

V: Doing what?

BG: Cutting stone.

V: For him, you mean—

BG: No, for *me.* He even gave me some pretty precious materials of one kind or another. He gave a very beautiful piece of marble once that he let me do what I wanted with… a few other things like that.

V: You did sculptures at that time, but none survived?

BG: No, not that I know of.

V: Did you start to think at that time what the *purpose* of "art" might be? Was it just "play" for you?

BG: No. I began to think of it in sort of Marxist terms, being essentially a part of the panoply of the upper classes—being an element of conspicuous consumption.

V: John Berger has done a lot of dissemination of the idea of the history of art being the history of conspicuous consumption. He did a series of videos. He's done several books tracing that idea, illustrating, documenting...

BG: That's a very 1930s way of thinking. Marxism was taught in the most expensive schools.

V: No kidding? Well, this is pre-World War Two—a totally different era.

BG: On the one hand it produced those traitors like Burgess and Maclean and Philby [the Cambridge Spy Ring, Cambridge students recruited as Soviet spies in the 1930s], and many more that have still never been discovered. It got into everybody's thinking in a way, along with psychoanalysis.

Freudianism was much less taught—certainly, in Catholic school, there was a fair level of that, but Marxism managed to get its dirty little snout in there quite a bit. It came out like a gas.

I left school—I fucked up on a scholarship to Oxford. I went to Oxford and wrote exams there and decided it was a hateful place and not for me at all. I decided I wanted to come to Paris and go to the Sorbonne, which I did by the time I was 18.

I was drawing a lot just for my own, I suppose, *psychic satisfaction*. Rather sadistic, or I suppose masochistic... abstract. I was very interested in the abstract movement at the time; the De Stijl, echo of the Bauhaus—which didn't really come on until 1932, 1934. Klee left Germany about 1932? Others did too. It really wasn't until Hitler got into full swing there that he managed to clear them all out, and they scattered all over Europe and went to America, too.

When I arrived in Paris, it was Freud who had the starring role much more than Marx, who was considered old-fashioned, dangerous and grubby. Whereas Freud was smart and well-connected, being taught at universities already. It was exciting that he had been a continuation of [Jean-Martin] Charcot who had these large public exhibitions of throwing people into fits of epilepsy. Well, they were considered *ecstasy*.

I met this Greek. He was very pushy, himself, and sort of trailing me along behind him. He introduced me to the Surrealist group, saying, "You must show them your drawings! You must see his drawings!" And really grudgingly I pulled out what were meant to be *notebooks*—not art books, but notebooks that had drawings and things in them. Everyone said, "Ooh, that's very interesting."

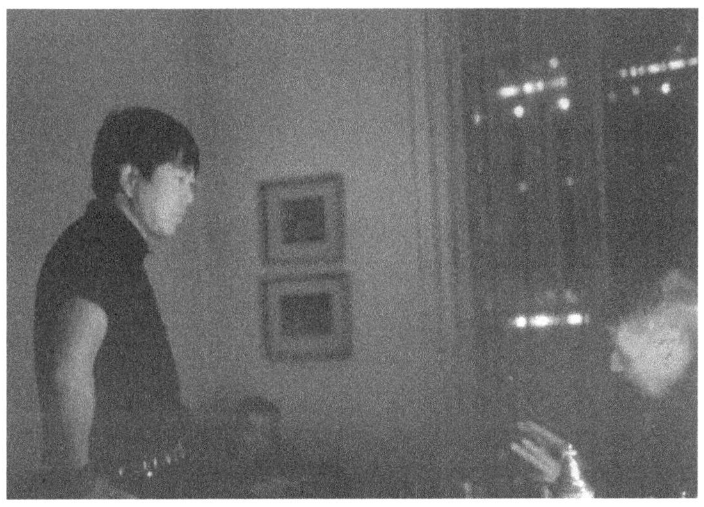

V. Vale and Brion Gysin, Paris

V: Automatic writing, eh?

BG: All of that sort of thing, yeah. I was saying, "No, no, I had nothing to do with those abstract people; they're completely wrong, they just don't understand at all." Surrealism was very glamorous, very social, very connected with dressmaking and rich people and smashing parties—

V: At least at this time. We're talking '32, around there. Yeah, it had already broken through, because the first Surrealist manifestos were 1924 or—

BG: Yeah, then they had managed to take over Dada.

V: And they tried to humiliate Dada—

BG: And they did—they humiliated the shit out of Tristan Tzara. They accused him of being a fink and a police informer; all kinds of things they laid on him. It was a terrorist group on its way to power—

V: —with the aid of high-society ladies, right?

BG: Lots of dressmakers, and ladies who went to those dressmakers.

V: So, Brion, you were introduced by a Greek—this wasn't Nicolas Calas, was it?

BG: I don't know. [cagily]

V: You don't know the name of this person?! The only Greeks I can think of that were connected with Surrealism were—

BG: You know him?

V: I don't *know* him, but he's quite well-known, and then there is—

BG: Who's he well-known *to?*

V: I don't know, I just thought he was famous—a writer, etc. And Nanos Valaoritis. He's a Greek Surrealist poet, but he wasn't involved until later.

BG: What do you mean by "later"?

V: Fifties-sixties. He knows people like Lebel, people like that. Robert Lebel, not Jean-Jacques. He's much later, whereas you're talking about the early thirties. Go ahead, don't let *me* talk! They took you to the galleries, and you met people like Max Ernst. He was in Paris then—

BG: Oh yeah, he was married to Marie-Berthe Aurenche—that was his second wife. She let me into his studio.

V: Do you remember where it was?

BG: Rue des Plantes. He was doing rubbings. I had only two art lessons and that was one and it took about two minutes. I said, "Migod, of course that's it—you make the painting make itself." You don't go fiddling away, *adding,* or all this business of sort of artsy-crafty nonsense. You just let the fucker make itself.

At the same time, I met Leonor Fini, and she gave me rather *contrary* advice about what was traditional: "how to make the salad." How much vinegar to put into the oil to whip up emotion and make your fucking salad. She's *still* making salads; her pictures are all salads. That led me astray for a while, into painting *meticulously* and trying to imitate.

V: You just mentioned you had a notebook of drawings, but you'd picked up a brush at some point?

BG: No, if I'd just gone back elsewhere I would have picked up nothing but a brick!

V: [laughs] Stone.

BG: Then Leonor said, "No, no, you must use a brush, and Max says 'all right.' But he's really a gym instructor, he's not a painter at all."

She was having an affair, fucking him, and she said, "Yeah, he was a 1, 2, 3, 4... 1, 2, 3, 4... 1, 2, 3, 4... very dramatic. He's a gym instructor."

V: *That's* what Leonor Fini said about Max Ernst?!

BG: Yeah.

V: This *is* Leonor Fini you're talking about. He also had an affair with Leonora Carrington, but later.

BG: No, it was almost simultaneous. Two crazy ladies at once was not too much for Max!

V: Yeah, she *really* went mad. Unlike Fini. Fini kind of kept it together. You knew Leonora Carrington?!? Let's put it this way: you met her. How would you describe her? Give me some impressions.

BG: Dirty girl.

V: A what?

BG: A dirty girl! She looked like an unmade bed.

V: God, she's one of my favorites. Favorite painters, that is.

BG: She was a grubby girl, not very clean.

V: But, hard-working?

BG: No, running around and being very Irish, you know. Mad thing! Being sort of *Wuthering Heights.* She thought she was Cathy or something, and in fact didn't Balthus do a whole series of drawings of her as Cathy?

V: Oh, I've seen all the drawings, but I didn't know they were modeled on *HER*. Wow, those are great drawings. Balthus is one of my favorites, too.

BG: She was around in those days.

V: Well, you got to at least meet some of the major Surrealists of that time.

BG: Look at that list that I exhibited with—I knew every one of them. Look at that list again. You didn't read it today.

V: Well, sometimes just because you exhibit with them doesn't mean you actually *knew* them.

BG: Of course I knew them. *Migod,* you had to know them. You had to see them every day and pay the proper respects to each one.

V: Did you ever discuss theory of any kind?

BG: You'd sit down and be discussing the group pictures together.

V: You actually did some. With who?

BG: Oh, I don't know. Everybody. Exquisite cadavers. It was a terrorist organization. Those were its organizational techniques. You had to meet every so often.

V: Where? The Cafe Deux Magots?

BG: De Flore, which was not a faggot cafe in those days. Deux Magots was sort of *too serious*.

V: Well, did you have any discussions with any of them on theory of creativity?

BG: Oh, yes. Yelling and screaming.

V: Do you think it changed you? Influenced you?

BG: Well, I was very much against it.

V: Against? What ideas were you against, specifically?

BG: Their ideas on sex were incredible.

V: That's right. René Crevel was the only one—

BG: Well, they drove him to suicide—

V: Oh, I didn't know they *drove* him. Tell me all you know about René Crevel!

BG: I know very little.

V: That was before your time.

BG: No, no I went with him to get his hair cut on Sunday, and he committed suicide on Monday. Yeah, beautiful cat.

V: Can you recall any conversations? I'm interested in him.

BG: Well, it was rather horrible, actually. He was ordered to take on an official mistress to prove he was not homosexual, so he had this liaison with a wife of a Spanish ambassador. Her son had been my "fag" at school: the boy who made tea for me and stoked my fire, filled up my fireplace and blacked my boots and carried my gym togs from the gym to the swimming pool and cleaned the mud from my boots. That was the whole system of school in those days: *serfs.* [laughs] He was a very attractive boy; I had a photograph of him until very recently.

I was appalled and horrified and shocked and bewildered by this strange thing that was going on in Paris with Crevel. His mother was a very charming woman. I saw her again during the war and invited her to a party—I used to give a lot of parties in those days: 1940, '41 in *New York.* She met this wonderful woman named Iris Barry who invented the whole idea of cinematheques, who was in charge of the films at the Museum of Modern Art, and was English. Iris Barry had had a hard time, she had been a movie critic and had a long past that I didn't know much about. She even had a child by Wyndham Lewis—maybe she had *two* children by Wyndham Lewis—yeah, "*Two* many," everybody said. It was all very—what's the proper word for it? A nasty, sexy atmosphere that they tried to create—

V: —the Surrealists, you mean? Well: *Mad Love*, you know. *Nadja*—

BG: "Mad love" indeed. What a creep. It was all very incestuous. It seemed so strange that I had been with this faggot at school whose mother was parading around pretending to be a mistress to Crevel, and Crevel was driven to suicide. I refused to go to his funeral,

I remember, because it was held by the Communist party. They covered him with red roses, which was very grave. Must have been on a Thursday or a Friday, I guess.

There were a lot more incestuous carrying-ons than that; it was very creepy and unpleasant, a very sick sexual atmosphere. Public statements, some of which have come up and been republished. They were always having (or pretending to have) gang-bangs which I certainly never wanted to get mixed up in.

V: Really? I never heard of that.

BG: Could have been pretending, could have been real. Then they went out and did things like the "public rose" where Breton and Éluard went out, each with a rose and gave it to a girl he found on the street in Montmartre and married her. One of them was, what was her name? She was an acrobat in a small circus in Montmartre.

V: Simone Breton.

BG: No, no before her. Long before her. I remember she was kind of nice; she always had a trapeze she took around. I used to go and visit her.

V: Wait, this is one of Breton's wives?

BG: This is *one* of the wives. This is the mother of Aube [Jacqueline Lamba].

V: Is that Breton's only living daughter? That's the only daughter he had, I think.

BG: And Éluard married Nusch. It was on the sidewalks.

V: Oh.

BG: This was all considered to be very Surrealist.

V: They just took roses and married the first woman that appealed to them? It's that easy?

BG: But, everybody thought that the real couple was Éluard and Breton. The two of them were obviously lovers.

V: [laughs] That sounds like sheer heresy.

BG: Yeah, well they would have yelled and screamed and denied it, but it certainly looked that way to everybody else. We'd studied a little Freud on the side.

V: So, Gala hadn't entered the scene yet.

BG: Oh, yes she had. She's been in and out a couple of times. She's come in and plucked off young Mickey Mouse Dali by that time.

V: Yeah, 'cuz before she had been with Éluard and then Éluard went with Nusch, is that it?

BG: With whom?

V: Nusch.

BG: Was it that quick? Hadn't she been with Max Ernst between?

V: Really, Gala, you mean? Oh, I see. Perhaps.

BG: She's resting happily in Dali's stomach. He promised years ago that when she died that he would eat her, so of course for two years he's shut up in the little castle that she died in. Nobody went to the funeral and then he had that trouble with the fire and everything else, so we all considered that he must have finally finished her off.

V: He must have eaten her? I never heard that.

BG: This is a public boast, it's no invention of mine. She was a tough bird too, believe me. It'd take a lot of digesting.

V: [laughs]

BG: What a wicked, nasty woman—wow.

V: So did you ever meet Yves Tanguy?

BG: Oh, sure. He was a much more reasonable sort of person; he'd been a sailor. I remember going out with him several times and having a good time. He was about the only one of them I ever did have a good time with—he was nice. Then he married that American, ex-Princess. What's her name?

V: Kay Sage.

BG: She had been married to an Italian Prince.

V: Actually, I like her paintings as well.

BG: Really?

V: I've only seen a couple.

BG: No opinion, no opinion. We had this big fuss over the show in December. Friday the 13th of December 1935 was the day that I arrived at 5:30 to see how my pictures had been hung, and I found everyone unhanging them and saying that it was the orders of Breton to unhang

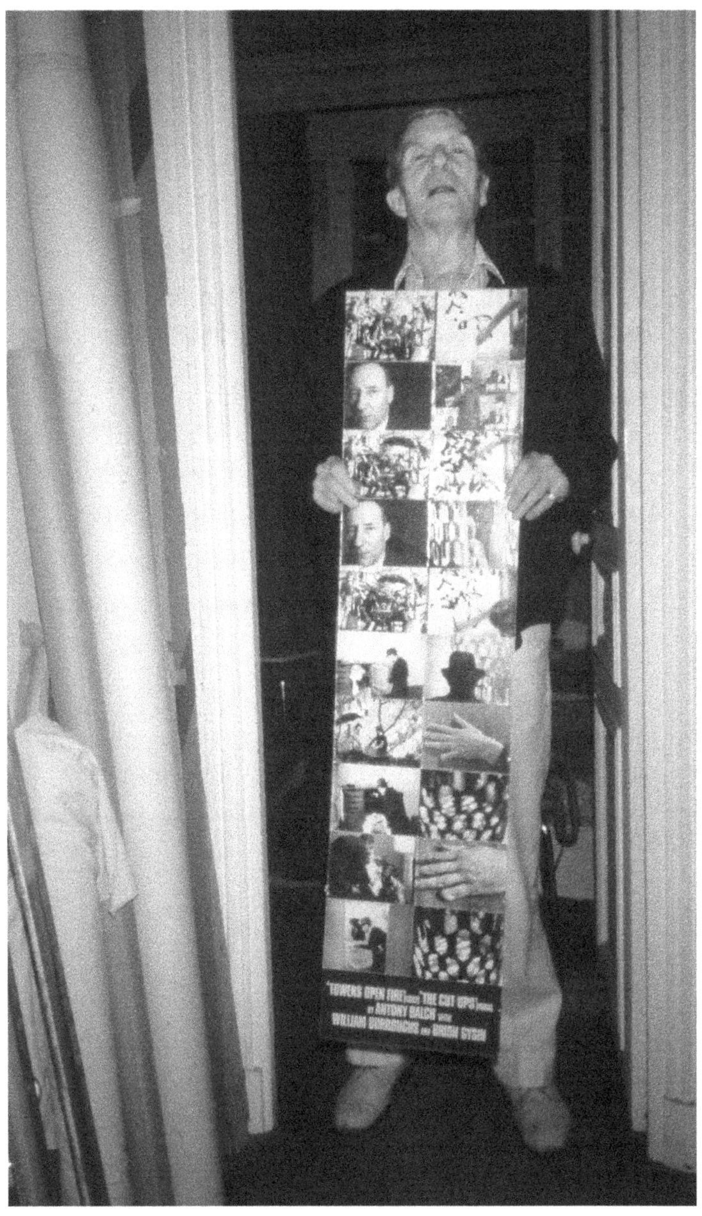

Brion Gysin holding a movie poster for The Cut Ups

them. I said, "Why?" and they said, "Don't know." I was with Valentine Hugo, who had previously been a mistress of Breton's and was on very bad terms with him.

V: I just bought her book of paintings.

BG: Really? What's it look like?

V: It's beautiful. It looks older to me, but the truth is I haven't even looked at it yet. I just picked it up last night in a store.

BG: I see. Well, she was sort of a *technician* in her way: *Dot, dot, dot.*

V: A very romantic technician!

BG: She was a very nice woman. (I suppose you read, some years ago, that the correspondence between her and I had been sold at public auction?) I guess it must have been just *after* this; they must have thanked her for her "intervention" (or whatever it was). I remember after this all happened we all went out to dinner together.

V: She took you to dinner.

BG: Obviously, I wasn't taking *her* to dinner.

[break in recording]

...at least two patients, maybe even more than that—the tips of their penises have been cut off. Sickly blind, blind Rabbis—

V: —doing the circumcision? It's barbaric.

BG: You know, they do it at the age of six days, so there

isn't really much to work with—you'd *better* have sharp eyes.

X: In America, they just do it when you're born; they don't wait six days.

BG: No? I remember perfectly, it was done to punish me. I was told by these ladies if I didn't quit touching myself, I would have my little penis cut off! So I had to be operated on for "tonsils." I woke up in a pool of blood.

X: How old were you?

BG: Five, and I've never forgiven them for this.

V: What ladies were this? Your mother among them?

BG: Mother, aunt, grandmother. [Stella Martin Gysin, Clare Martin, Margaret Martin]

X: You never called her "mommy" again?

BG: No, never.

X: You called her "mother"?

BG: Yep.

X: Cruel punishment.

V: Cruel and unusual.

BG: When she got married again I called her "Mrs. Hugall." [Hewgill]

X: You did? That's funny.

BG: It wasn't funny for her. She was a very admirable woman; she's a saint in Vancouver. All that gang on the Western Front. Everybody from up and down the West Coast, when they went to Vancouver (which they didn't do very much in those days, but they did more and more), used to stop in there. Allen Ginsberg spent two weeks there, pumping her for information every night, she said.

V: When was this? The fifties?

BG: When he came to India by way of Japan.

V: Around '63?

BG: About then. She always had a big open house, for poets and people like that. It got her into plenty of trouble, you can imagine…

X: I just got this *Pauper's Paris* book—

BG: Poppers? Who's got poppers?

V: You don't take those, do you Brion?

BG: Not in a long time, but I wouldn't mind one tonight.

V: It might send you through the ceiling.

BG: That's what I need.

V: No, you don't. It's 7:20 now. Just for my own curiosity, I must ask you about a few other Surrealists. I like Dorothea Tanning's work a lot, so if you could recall anything: when you met her, what you might have talked about, things like that—

BG: This is all scandalous gossip.

V: Well, it's interesting to me for personal reasons.

BG: All I can tell you is Peggy Guggenheim talked of her as "that thief."

V: Dorothea Tanning?

BG: "Yeah, she stole Max away from me, the one great love of my life! Love thief, yes, she's a love thief." You know, kind of a giddy old girl, a very Surrealist lady painter.

V: Yeah.

BG: She's all right. Okay, an old friend.

V: I'm trying to flesh out the years when the Greek introduced you to the Surrealists, until the time Éluard took down your paintings in '35.

BG: I met that whole gang of "no-goods" in late 1934, and the exhibition took place in December 13-31, 1935. [Galerie Aux Quatre Chemins, 99 Boulevard Raspail, Paris VI, France]

V: So it was one year you spent.

BG: I didn't see much of them all. I saw quite a different group of painters—like Balthus. There were people who called themselves Neo-Romantics (or something like that) at that time, who were much nicer and quieter people and not personal or sexual or social disasters like all the Surrealists prided themselves on being. I saw a whole different gang of people. A lot of paintings done in that period have disappeared completely… Not all.

I'll tell you what happened to a lot of pictures. I

had a few years of being very, very social: all sorts of old school friends and connections from old school friends. You know how if you were young and charming it was quite easy to meet people who were giving parties and were delighted to have you come to them. So I went to an awful lot of parties between 1935 and 1939.

V: This was all in Paris—

BG: Paris, yeah. Then after a particularly social season after the Spring of 1939, I decided I simply had to go away by myself and decide what the fuck was going on. I went down to Arles and this particular friend of mine who had introduced me to a lot of grand people—

V: Who was that?

BG: An Italian friend.

V: What was his name? [Giovanni Stagni?]

BG: No need to drag him into it, he was just a very good-looking, very handsome, very fashionable boy who spent most of his time becoming intimate with the Royals. He knew all the ex-kings and queens and people like that who were still giving parties. I said, "I can't stand any more of this, I'm going away by myself." He found where I was and told me the one thing that would get me to come and join him, which was the Spanish Republic, with whom I had an enormous amount of sympathy, me even sending all my winter clothes to them and things like that, walking around in skinny summer suits.

They had hocked all of the pictures of the Prado to a bank in Switzerland, and by 1939, the bank had figured that their cause was lost. They had told them: either they had to pay their enormous debts, or their pictures would be sold at public auction. He said this may be the last chance in the world to see the pictures together because it was his bank and his father's bank. Everybody who was interested in that sort of thing, a most disparate group of people, made enormous efforts to get there to this show. I thought, "I guess if I can hock my bicycle I can make it there on the train and get there with an overnight bag. I'll be back inside a week."

Of course, I never got back because war was declared in a period of about ten days or so! I rather luckily found myself in Switzerland, but everything I owned in the world, which was mostly pictures I guess, was left behind in Paris and a lot of it was left in a gallery, luckily.

After my quarrel with the Surrealists over this exhibition, the gallery too quarreled with them over the way they treated me, which was rather unexpectedly loyal of them. The gallery was really not quite right for the Surrealists in any case. They were having this show of just drawings in 1935.

That was the first group show there ever was, but in 1938 they had their painting exhibition at [Galerie Beaux-Arts], which was on the other side of the river, near the Presidents' Palace there. That is where Dali had the taxi where it rained inside—it didn't rain outside the taxi, it only rained *inside* the taxi! Those cutesy tricks they were up to! Some of the historical books consider that the first Surrealist exhibition... the very first group exhibition that there was, with all of those very famous names. They're world-famous and worth a lot of money... except mine.

The gallery wasn't quite right for them; the gallery really liked the Neo-Romantics—all those now-quite-forgotten painters, but who were big moneymakers in those days—very fashionable. The gallery then moved from Montparnasse, where the show had been, to Champs-Élysées which was *chic-er,* and they offered me a show there in May 1939. Most of the pictures that I had were shown in that gallery. Quite a few were sold, which made it possible for me to go off by myself like that. And the rest stayed there during the entire war. I found them again in 1949, ten years later.

V: In Paris?

BG: The same gallery. I had a friend, a rather difficult friend, and a difficult patron who was a brother of Hans Richter. You know him?

V: Yeah, of course.

BG: Well, his brother Albert preferred to call himself Albert Rothschild. It sounded like more money. In that German way, even Swiss way, you use your father's name and then your mother's name after it. Hans Richter preferred just to call himself Hans Richter and his brother Albert chose to call himself Albert Rothschild. Albert came with me, and I had no place to put these pictures, and Albert goes, "Oh, I'll put these in my house!" Not that he bought every single one of them or anything, but I really had no other place to put them. By that time I was in an entirely new life in Paris as a Fulbright fellow studying the history of slavery. I wasn't parading as a painter at all.

V: Wait, did we just skip over ten years?

BG: Well, yeah. That's all—I mean—WAR.

V: World War II. You actually saw combat and all that?

BG: No, no. I saw three armies and no combat. Except internal combat. I was in three armies, and I loved all of them.

V: What were they?

BG: I was in the British Army, the Canadian Army, and the American Army.

V: How the hell did that happen?

BG: We needn't go into that.

V: Okay, let's skip that for now.

BG: That gets a little complex. I adore the army. I had a very good time there because you have perfect freedom. You don't have to worry about eating or sleeping or being housed or traveling or anything. You're just completely, completely free and in exchange for this you give up your liberty. And they give you some liberty back every once in a while: a weekend here and two weeks there. (In the Navy in America, they call it liberty.) So it's a very fair exchange, I found. As I'd

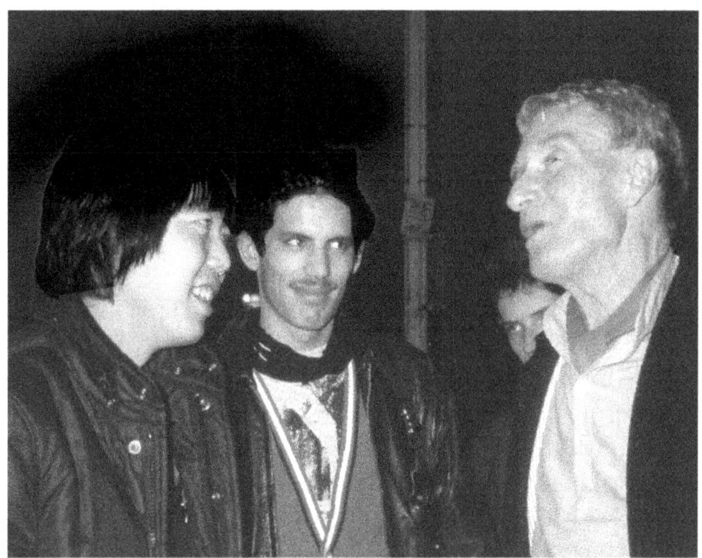

V. Vale, David Wells and Brion Gysin at the Final Academy, London, 1982

gone to officer training school in England, I found it all very understandable.

V: So that would explain why you produced hardly any art between 1939 and 1949—

BG: A pretty fair explanation, I must add. However, I had done a whole lot of other things. I worked on seven big Broadway musicals where I was the assistant costume designer. I worked on *Banjo Eyes*, *Lady in the Dark*, *Sunny River*, *New Faces 1941, By Jupiter*—all of them, a whole bunch. Yeah, I did a lot of things actually. That's how I still had Broadway connections when I wrote my *Uncle Tom* book. Everybody said, "Man, you got all the material for a musical here." That's jumping ahead a little bit. Where are we? What year?

V: 1949.

BG: I went back to Paris on my Fulbright fellowship as a *historian,* writing the history of slavery—not as a painter. It was an accident that I even *asked* for a Fulbright—the whole thing was run by a bunch of queens who told me, "My dear, we chose you by your photograph." I said, "Well, thanks, pals."

The photograph had been taken very much on purpose by a Bachrach—a society photographer from New York who used to take photographs of successful young people. *That* got me my Fulbright! "This looks like Fulbright material," they said. Little did they know.

Anyhow, I got back together with "Albert Rothschild," and he got all of my pictures exchanged for some quite minor kindnesses really, but an awful lot of attention. He died a few years ago and I have only Gregory Corso's word for it. What kind of word is that?

Gregory says he saw an account in the newspaper which he forgot to clip out, saying Albert Rothschild's pictures had been sold at a public auction, naming or numbering 15 to 20 of mine.

So they have been scattered at auctions. I wrote to his widow, and she knew nothing about it, but she did understand what had happened. He died in New York, and all kinds of people immediately invaded the house and carried things off. This always happens to people who live rather open, complicated social lives—they're rather open to being *pillaged*. You know: the decorator comes, and little friends come…

All of those pictures from 1935 to 1939 are scattered around in America, under what name, or what guise or what price I have no idea, and I have no photographs of any of them. The only things that I have are the ones I showed you today, which were watercolor on paper or decalcomania on paper. But all the oils have gone.

V: So you had done oils? Oh, yeah. You started around '34.

BG: Well, '34, '35, yeah. I was misled, I was utterly misled by all the good advice. If I had really stuck to what I thought, I would have been a minor (because they're all sort of "minor") abstract painter from the thirties. I did cones and pyramids and circles and things. I translated that very much to real things like light coming through a portal on a ship, being the cone of light and the source being the portal and going round and round being on another plane. Stuff like that interested me: *the mechanics of paintings.* Then I got pulled into that sloppy folklore of Surrealism—

V: What do you mean by "sloppy folklore"?

BG: Well, that's just what it is, you know. People looking like birds. Feathers all over their asses and that sort of thing. Tables that look like dogs.

V: Did you ever meet Victor Brauner?

BG: Yeah. Thank God I didn't go to that party.

V: Domínguez—

BG: Yeah, where Domínguez put out Brauner's eye.

V: We're back to Paris, 1949, still.

BG: No.

V: 1950 then.

BG: No, we're not in Paris in 1950. I didn't see Brauner and all those people by then. I cut off all relations with the Surrealists after the shitting on me in 1935.

V: After Breton's little act. Just because he did that, didn't mean you couldn't ever speak to Valentine Hugo ever again.

BG: No, but she was already out. She was a dissident.

V: She was a declared dissident? They didn't kick her out?

BG: I don't know.

V: As far as I know they didn't. They weren't so hard on the women.

BG: No, no, 'cuz she had more money. I mean she'd married Hugo [descendant of Victor Hugo] after all. A good name and stuff like that. They never attacked anyone, except people that were defenseless. Breton was a terrific coward.

V: In what way?

BG: He was a piece of slime, man, he was a real piece of slime. A terrorist, an organizer of a terrorist group with all of the techniques that you would employ to keep such a sort of *cult* together. So, I saw them again in New York. They had a very hard time getting to America. They'd all gone off on one boat like the Ark from Marseilles. Peggy Guggenheim had gone down there and bought a lot of pictures very quickly. She bought all her collection.

V: Didn't Breton cross the Atlantic in the same boat with Claude Lévi-Strauss?

BG: They were all together in Marseilles. Peggy made a raid down there. She had the only ready cash money that anybody had. So she bought her whole collection of paintings for, she once told me (it's hard to believe) something under $5,000. She bought all of her pictures in a matter of two or three days.

V: In her collection, you mean?

BG: Yeah. She went around: *bam, bam, bam.* That didn't include, of course, big Max Ernsts she got off him later—no, payment for marrying him and getting him out of Ellis Island. She got all *those* paintings for very little money.

They needed every little penny they had and that all got them on this one boat which took them to Martinique. In Martinique, there was a Vichy admiral whose name we've all forgotten (I hope) who put them in a concentration camp. So the first news one had in New York in 1940 was that they were all in this camp.

I felt sorry for them because I had quite big studios around the corner of 56th and Madison. Three, really, 'cuz I'd loaned one to somebody. I figured there was no point carrying the quarrels of the old world into the new one as they were all quite helpless, none of them speaking a word of English. I thought, "Well, might as well," so I did a second round with them.

V: Oh, with, like, Breton and people?

BG: Yeah, even Breton.

V: Can you think of more Surrealists you may have associated with?

BG: Well, yeah. It was at that time that I first met Roberto Matta. In the interim, he had popped up from Chile and Spain and joined the group. I met him in 1940; I was living on Washington Square and he was living down on McDougall Street. There were some boys that we knew that had been picked up by a couple of other painters like that who were models. We used to draw all night in front of the models. It doesn't sound either like him or me, but we did.

V: It doesn't sound like Matta, especially in light of what he paints.

BG: It's all based on human anatomy, really.

V: Sort of.

BG: Oh, sure.

V: *Psychic* human anatomy.

BG: They're sort of comic strip characters. A science-fiction of comic-strip characters.

V: That's a funny way to describe a Matta work like "Invasion of the Night"—the painting I've seen the most in San Francisco at SF Museum of Modern Art.

BG: Yeah.

V: He spoke English?

BG: I don't think so. I spoke Spanish.

V: I quite like his work, actually.

BG: He's going to have a big show next fall here.

V: Was he finally really famous, or what? There aren't any big books available. Only little, small ones.

BG: No. Well, it's all going to be fixed now; his present wife is arranging all that. She's very wealthy. She owns a pharmaceutical firm; her and her brother know business. He's taught all of his wives the art business. He's got a whole bunch of widows looking after his future, you see. Six, seven.

V: He's had that many wives?

BG: Yeah. They're all good working girls. He's taught them the whole business from the ground up. He's had an awful lot of troubles, too, you know. Moving around too much, never stopping too long in one place. A lot of the mistakes I made in my day, changing nationality... just like me, he's done all of it.

V: You never happened to meet Wifredo Lam?

BG: Yeah, yeah. He was a very nice man.

V: Does he live here, or did he?

BG: He died here; he lived here and he died here. I never

was intimate with him; I only knew him from a distance. I met him once or twice in the Matisses' house in New York all those years ago. Then I saw him at his farewell; he appeared in a wheelchair. Musicians there played—

V: Cuban music?

BG: A very touching evening. He had financial troubles, too. A couple of wives, terrible tax problems. Nobody is really—no big, big merchant is defending him, as they say.

V: So, we're in 1950 now?

BG: I was back here in 1950. I had hardly really been back to New York since then. I missed the whole scene.

V: '49 Paris, '50, still Paris.

BG: Paris and Spain.

V: '49, you're taking up painting again.

BG: No, in '49 I'm a historian back here writing the definitive history of slavery.

V: Which you wrote in Paris.

BG: No, I didn't write it, ever! Nobody could. I became almost immediately unpopular in academic circles.

V: For the book?

BG: Yeah, because I said I was going to write a book called *The Future of Slavery.*

V: [laughs]

BG: So obviously that is the future, as sure as any.

V: Where does this tie in with research you were going to do in the south of France with all these documents you had about slavery? This was the same time, right?

BG: Bordeaux, yeah, a big sailing family that's still down there in the wine business, and in trade in general. The best trade there ever was.

V: Okay, you're back in Paris in '50. We seem to have stopped there.

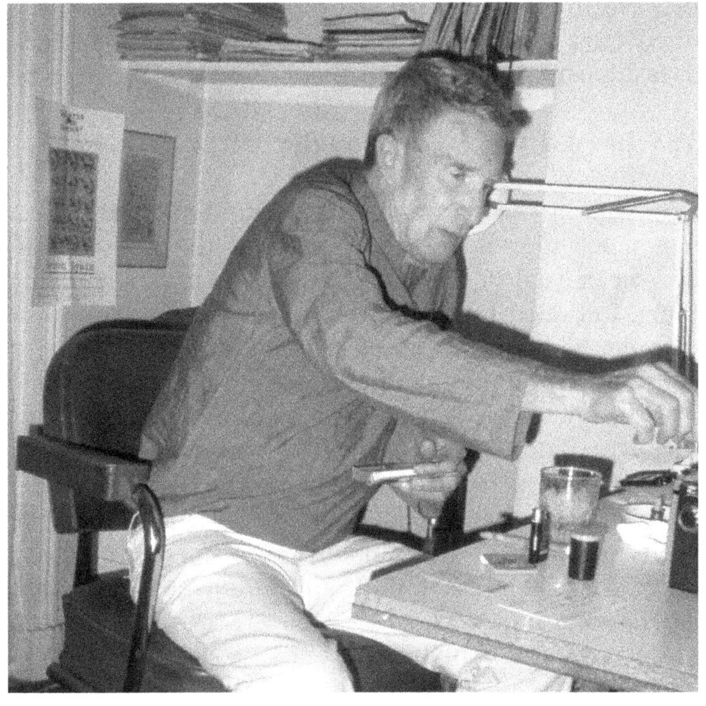

Brion Gysin at his apartment in Paris

BG: I went to the University of Bordeaux, and then I was connected to the Sorbonne through '49 and '50, and then I discovered the Indies and Seville. It was an easy little airplane ride between Seville and Tétouan in Morocco. So I went back and forth every weekend.

V: Had you met Paul Bowles before this?

BG: Yeah, way back in the thirties. I saw him during the forties in New York. West 10th Street. I eventually stayed in Tétouan for 23 years. Not in Tétouan. Tangiers, actually—

V: —where you discovered the smoking of hash?

BG: No, I didn't; I discovered that long before that. I discovered that in Greece in the 1930s. It wasn't nearly as fashionable then as it's become now. A downtown vice.

V: What did you get done in Seville?

BG: Nothing really constructive. I found that the subject was much too vast to begin. None of the archives had even been cataloged, even. There was no way of studying them. I decided I would just look into the papers called *asientos,* which were papers given by the royal court, by the king, in fact, to people, giving them the right to trade in so many slaves. I mean, you could buy an *asiento* for three slaves or for three hundred slaves or three thousand slaves. These papers then became a kind of money and were exchanged and bought and resold without even the human meat to go with them until they became rather like *assignats* during the French revolution—paper money. That's what I thought.

I started totaling up the ones I could find in these archives. When I started totaling them up in the millions I thought, "Well obviously, there is a mistake here." But it wasn't a mistake. They really did steal that many people.

V: Millions of people?

BG: Oh, millions of people.

V: From Africa.

BG: The death rate was 50, 60 and 100 percent.

V: I read this book called *Black Cargoes*.

BG: Whose was that?

V: Daniel P. Mannix.

BG: There is a very good one written by a boy I went to school with called *Sins of the Fathers*. His great-grandfather had been one of the British governors down on the African coast, so he had access to the family papers of several families—the sort of people who built themselves big country houses in big rolling estates. When it all came out, it more than embarrassed them that anyone had found out this came from the slave trade... but it did. He had his fingers on those papers.

He and I must have talked about this at school, looking back on it all. He was murdered, so I never had a chance to *really* discuss this in great length with him. He was called James Pope-Hennessy. His brother John Pope-Hennessy is the head of the Victoria & Albert Museum, Florence Flood Relief, and all those other big art swindles. Sir John Pope-Hennessy.

We had a school magazine called *The Raven*. John was the editor in '32 and I guess I was the editor in '34. In '35 James, the younger brother, took it over. So one of them ended in the way that I've described in fiction, except that's actually what happened to him [James was murdered on 25 January 1974]. If you send a boy out to shop in the night, that's a mistake! John is one of the pillars of museology; keeper of the Queen's pictures. Anyhow, we're bleeding into gossip!

V: I'm actually trying to pick up this creative thread throughout all these travels and all these years and things. String 'em together.

BG: It's very simple: "Here's a passport."

V: [laughs]

BG: Write a book or two along the way.

V: When you are spending more time in Tétouan, it obviously influenced what you were doing creatively.

BG: Oh, I learned everything I know there! How to take a bath, how to wipe my ass, how to blow my nose, how to eat properly… *everything.*

V: You don't eat with your fingers, do you?

BG: Yeah, sure I do. Very well. Not as well as some of the Moroccan royal princesses that I've known, who can down an enormous amount of food! You would just think they were birds *fluttering* over the plate. I never learned how to do *that,* but I do it kind of *country-style.* You take a wad of couscous and you pop it right in with your thumb. I can do that… not many other Christians can claim as much!

Really, when I sum it up—and we may sum it up right now! When I count at my present age, it works out perfectly. I spent 23 years of my life in North America, 23 other years in Europe and 23 in North Africa.

Myself and William [Burroughs] were intimately

connected with cut-ups. William clipped out these things and the cut-up read, "It's a bad thing for a child to sue his own father." Then almost immediately one heard of the fact that a young Getty had sued J. Paul Getty. I met Robina [Lund, friend and legal advisor to Getty], who's the girl with piano legs who lived with an old man named J.P. She got $300 a month for her years of servitude, in his will. I gave her a copy of *Minutes to Go* with that thing underlined in it to take to the old man, and that was our first connection.

V: You just met her in a London bar?

BG: She was with a friend. She got nothing out of all that deal. Have you ever read anything about the accounts of the last days of old J. Paul? Big, fat, lousy ladies are wagging their cunts at him night and day hoping he would die in their arms! But he couldn't do anything else. Must have been really hard.

V: Do you think he died happy?

BG: **Nobody died happy.**

V: With a smile on his face?

BG: Nobody could wipe it off.

V: [laughs] 

4. RESTAURANT INTERVIEW (March 1985)

V: There was a Moroccan cookbook that came in at City Lights Bookstore and I'm not sure who did it: Hamri? What was the name of the chef at your restaurant, Hamri?

BG: No.

V: I think it was a limited edition; Ira Cohen might have had something to do with it. I didn't get it because I hadn't the slightest interest in cooking then; now I wish I had. What kind of food did Hamri make? Couscous?

BG: No, he's a very inventive cook, a genius cook.

V: So Moroccans use vegetables… they use carrots and potatoes and tomatoes…

BG: Except they're really good there.

V: What kind of spices do they use that we don't use? The whole range—

BG: Yes.

V: Is there a Moroccan restaurant in Paris? What's the name?

BG: Timgad.

V: We shoulda gone there!

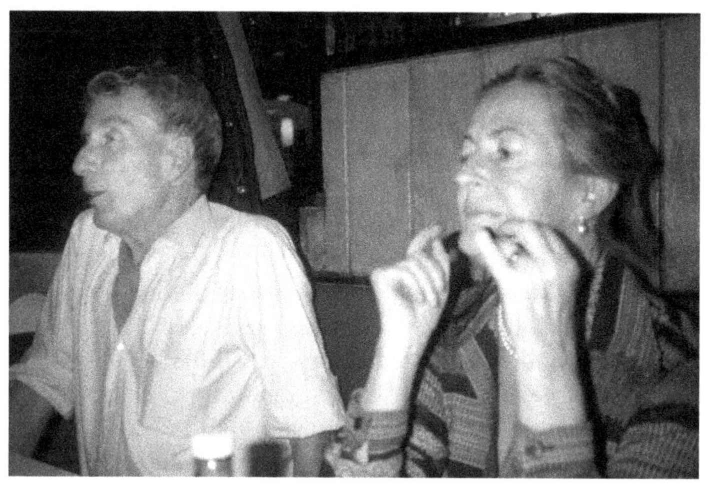

Brion Gysin and Felicity Mason at the Final Academy, London

BG: Too far!

V: They don't use curry in Morocco, do they?

BG: No, not much, no.... Is that a baked potato?

V: No, it's a lovely endive. There's some flavor in there that should be from Bali. Would you like a bite of it?

BG: No, thanks. It's a lovely shape and size and color.

V: I like the title of Felicity Mason's book [written under the pseudonym Anne Cumming], *The Love Habit*. A good habit is hard to kick; I think the sex habit is too—or is it the same?

BG: The same. And Felicity's still hunting them down; the toothless old lioness, yeah... some tender gay meat...

V: I must say, I like her a lot.

BG: Oh, I do too. She saved my life!

V: She has some good paintings of yours, too.

BG: Hasn't enough! I mean, considering all the things she's done for me. I crashed on her turf, after all. In England I had to be carried off the plane, claiming that I couldn't go on further. I was on my way to America when I had a homing instinct that had I been to America I would have just been shoveled into a bin. Because I had a hundred thousand dollars' worth or more of surgery and care and she arranged everything. She made a big play for my surgeon; she didn't realize that he was gay; she was going to *seduce* him! It was embarrassing. But he was a very nice man. A friend told me, "If you should happen to crash in England, look up this home network." So I just got in *under the wire* because they were changing the law about doing surgery to foreigners and *whatnot.* David Bowie helped too, but the Stones didn't raise a fuckin' finger for me.

V: I guess Bowie is actually a decent sort.

BG: Oh yes, very.

V: I've heard that from a bunch of people: he's actually a "real" guy; a workaholic...

[break in recording]

BG: ...They [*WHO* is Brion talking about here?!?] still had their full set of slaves there; eunuchs on the door, slavery in the kitchen, and they did a lot of the cooking for me—did all the pastry and stuff like that.

V: What did they make that was good?

BG: They just *make it better...* infinitely better.

V: They don't have slaves anymore, do they?

BG: Oh yes they do. The South still has slaves, after all.

V: The American South?

BG: Oh yeah. They can't get away. They're not allowed to buy and sell them in public anymore, but by custom and by habit and everything they can't get away. They don't WANT to get away!

V: You mean the "real" Uncle Toms?

BG: Yeah.

V: Has AIDS had much impact here? Michel Foucault died recently.

BG: Quite a few that I know have left us: a sculptor, an art dealer, a restaurant-keeper, etc. They don't talk about it much here... America loves to be scared; America loves to panic. Panic over rabies, scabies, herpes—anything like that: scary for a week. *Scare of the Week club*: those weekly magazines like *Time* and *Newsweek*.

V: Fear sells!

BG: AIDS is called SIDA here: same letters. People have remarked on the curious coincidence.

V: You know that French water called "Evian" is "naïve" spelled backward. Do you think that's a coincidence?

BG: Completely. It's a place name. 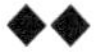

5. BRION GYSIN ON ART (March 7, 1985)

BG: Well, I knew I couldn't get to Hollywood anyhow, so I decided that I was going to be a welder. In a Bayonne, New Jersey high-school basement I learned how to weld, in a practical crash course that lasted from twelve o'clock at night until seven o'clock in the morning. I had to find my way home. My feet got as big as snowshoes, cracked open—

V: Why?

BG: The heat, and the staying out late and standing around… You would wear newspapers under your shirt… a T-shirt to hold the newspapers in, to keep the heat from going right through your chest!

V: Jeez… The primal creative process begins in bed. Okay, Brion, do you have any regular work habits? I mean, did you try to draw any certain time every day? Did you have any kind of routine or discipline?

BG: Discipline, no. I don't think so.

V: It seems like you've certainly churned out a lot of work.

BG: Yeah, I suppose.

V: How did you do it? You must have had at least an unconscious *modus operandi*—

BG: Oh, it was a pleasure, I guess. I never thought of it. I *hate* to work. The word "work"—I never employ it. I never *do* any, I think! It's just *play*.

V: Let's say that when you were doing Peggy Guggenheim's windows. Did you just more or less do them when you *felt* like it?

BG: Yeah, I guess.

V: What were your usual hours, though—are you a nocturnal person?

BG: No, not really. I never worked at night—if you call it "work". No.

V: When do you usually get up, through most of your life, or did it change? How about in Morocco... Tangiers?

BG: I don't know; I don't know. I don't think I am a very disciplined person by nature—**eat when you're hungry, sleep when you're tired. Draw when you feel like it; paint when you feel like it**... One can paint and listen to music, but I cannot write and listen to music. I used to *always* listen to music, and I still do quite a bit, but less. I listen to music continually... all my waking hours, I guess.

V: Music from what countries of origin?

BG: Oh, particularly Arab music—Moroccan music.

V: For the last thirty years?

BG: At this moment, thirty-five years.

V: Do you have any particular favorites?

BG: Oh yeah.

V: Can you name names?

BG: No, not really. You mean great *stars?!?*

V: I don't know... maybe unknown greats—unknown to most Westerners, that is? I mean, *everyone's* heard of Om Kalsoum.

BG: Yeah.

V: And there must be many more. Well, we just heard one *we* didn't even know who she was... different.

BG: She may be fairly new. There *are* a few new singers who are pretty good, but I don't really know them, or recognize any of them... [drily] Are you going to ask more precise questions?

V: Well...

BG: I don't think I was ever very disciplined. No.

V: Well, this is a *general* question... How do you get your ideas? How do you get your inspirations? I can't imagine suddenly getting an idea for a painting and *doing* it—my mind doesn't work that way. But it obviously has worked that way for *you!* How does it happen?

BG: I don't know. I haven't really kept... I have no idea.

V: You sit in front of a *tabula rasa* and then you just accidentally decide to pick "blue"? So you put some blue on the canvas or the paper?

BG: No, no, certainly not, it's really rather… theoretical, but I've never been very loquacious about my theories of… as I said earlier today. Some people *are*—they just *talk*—or at least they do more talking than anything else. I think I don't talk enough about how I work. I don't know.

V: One of the characteristics of your work is a very rapid, yet somehow precise, fluidity of motion.

BG: Yeah, well that comes from training oneself.

V: When did you develop this? You weren't *born* able to do these really fast. Did it get developed while you were studying Japanese? You don't learn that in school.

BG: No, that particular aspect of my work certainly came from my acquaintance with Japanese. The excellent teachers that we had were very unusual people who by force of circumstances in World War II became our teachers. They were not *academics* themselves. They were all very learned people in their way, and particularly the Japanese teachers were more acquainted with all of the theories behind writing… ***writing-as-painting*, which is very peculiarly Japanese, isn't it?**

V: Hmm… yeah… Was that the first time that you learned how to use a pen—did you use a sumi brush?

BG: I used only brushes; as a painter I was *acquainted* with brushes, but in a different way. 'Cuz *they* had a lot to say about the attack of the brush on the paper and the fluidity and the life in the *ink itself* as it runs. I could say a lot of things about it, but I won't sound very…

Take a famous old phrase like "who runs may read." I don't know where that comes from—perhaps the Bible or something; I have no idea. But I added to that: **"Read**

faster in order to run better"... *inverting* obviously *potent* ideas... almost part of my *brush*.

I don't know what most people do, 'cuz I never went to any sort of art school. So I really haven't got any "standards" except my own. I've never set *foot* in an art academy—I cannot imagine what they teach in there, any more than I've been to any schools of writing. It seems an amusing idea.

William [Burroughs] gave some lectures on the *technology of writing*, and a good deal of what he said and promulgated came out of long discussions that he and I had had on that subject.

But as far as art schools go, I have no idea what they can possibly teach. Maybe they teach things which are *very* useful!

V: Yeah, like how to mix paints.

BG: Shortcuts, like how to stretch a canvas, or where to buy the right kind of colors. I don't know *what* they do.

V: That's right—you get your inks from where?

BG: Sennelier. It's a very old 19th-century firm here in Paris. They make their colors and inks every day. They and the Ferme du Fonee [sic] are perhaps the only two people who still do make their own colors—they're not mass-produced. In fact, you have to order them in advance, and then they make them *for* you.

V: Do they make them out of old recipes like crushed beetle wings and things?

BG: I don't know too much about that as a matter of fact: what they *do* use. But yes they *do* have their own quietly secret processes. Who knows? But... I learned an awful lot about those *black* inks from the Japanese language teachers that I had. The whole idea of grinding your own ink and…

Why are *you* interested in the creative process?

V: I suppose because I am *not* a painter. I'm still mystified by *how people do it.* Does that seem fair enough?

BG: Yes. Nowadays they just go to *school*, don't they, and learn how to…?

V: Most art that I see, I can trace back to whom they ripped off. I'm not interested in art like that. I would never do something like that. And then there's obviously a fair amount of art for which I can't find any precedent. I have no idea where the "Elephant of Celebes" came from, for example.

BG: Which?

V: The Max Ernst painting. There's probably quite a number of works I have no idea where they came from. Even a painter like Matta… I relate him a little bit to Wifredo Lam, although he's not *really* related, except that they both use biomorphic shapes.

BG: Yes.

V: But… I'm just amazed when different artists can be so instantly recognizable, and "be their own man" so to speak—

BG: Right, yeah. Well, that is the *proof*, isn't it?!

V: I favor the kind of art that obviously stands up to repeated viewing over the years. Let's take your Moroccan paintings, the ones that are on the walls there. Every time you look at them you see different

people, different faces, different combinations—and of course, if you could *own* one, you'd see all kinds of different kinds of colorations throughout the year (I imagine), depending on the *season* and the *time of day*... things like that. Those seem to be unique.

BG: Making all those people *appear* is a sort of magical process, truly, yes. There's a lot of *looking away*, I mean *I don't push them onto the surface.* I've developed a way of *writing them*, and writing about them makes them appear. 'Cuz they're all very *calligraphic.*

V: Do you do do it out of the corner of your eye, or with your eyes slightly blurred, or what? Because there are just so many thousands of really precise strokes in those. There don't seem to be too many mistakes! [laughs]

BG: No, no—never make any mistakes—

V: And they also evidence quite a technical mastery to my mind, because, like, some of the strokes in the bicycles are just so fine, like a one-hair brush kind of stroke.

BG: Yeah—

V: Would you say you painted those in a slight trance, or—?

BG: Yeah, really!

V: What was your state of mind; you were listening to music, perhaps?

BG: Yeah, a great deal; mm-hmm...

V: I don't see how you could do those—they're amazing; they're very complex, too. It seems like it took incredible concentration—

BG: Well, I lived in that whole world—I was *soaked* into it for so many years. That was the only thing I would—I stayed there because I saw something magical that was disappearing, was leaving, and has been pretty well *destroyed* by now by the advance of industrialization. It

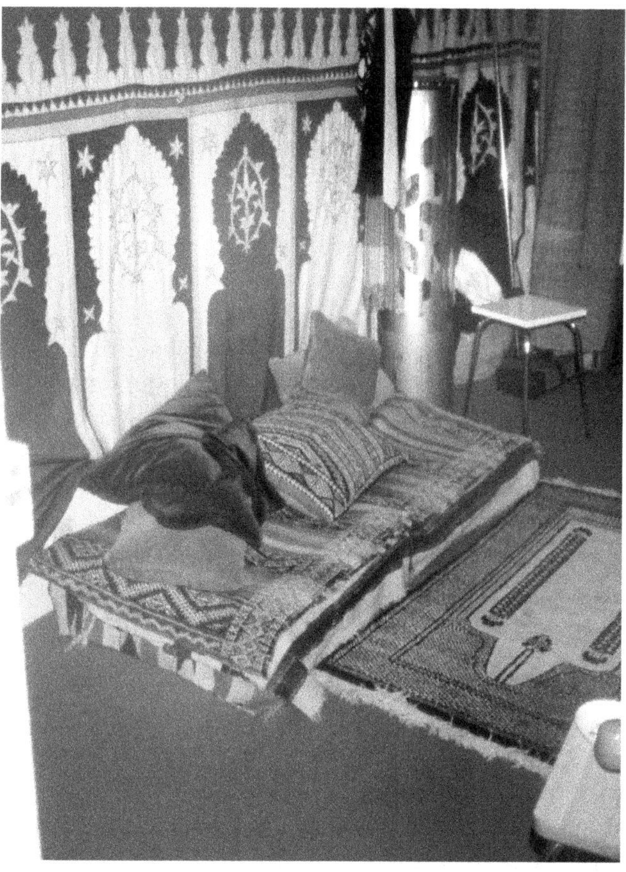

Brion Gysin's bedroom, with low bed and Moroccan fabrics

was a magic world that I saw at that time—it was very like living in the past—like truly living in Chaucer's time, let's say. That was before independence, previous to 1956, let's say. And since then, of course, it's been destroyed by…

Their music was destroyed, first of all, by the radio, and then even more so by the transistors; and a great deal… and then almost completely wiped out by television.

V: Oh, they've got TV there?

BG: Alas, yes.

V: Like four channels or something?

BG: I don't really know; I choose never to look at it, *anywhere*—not here, either! How many channels do they have here in Paris? I have no idea. I know *I* don't have one—not a single channel!

When I first went to North Africa in the 1930s, *everybody* could play music. In a café, the instruments would be hanging on the wall by a nail, and anybody who came along would pick them up and start playing them. And the radio changed *that*. But then in the country, everybody still played music at home, and the shepherd boys played their flutes in the hills. But then as soon as they got portable transistor radios, which they carried with them, they no longer played any instrument at all.

V: That's terrible.

BG: Well, this is inevitable, apparently—it's what we have done to the entire world, probably. It was a time of immense destruction—no *construction* at all! Many of the most beautiful things that the world has ever known are disappearing—like morning mist being burned off by the inventions of Western society. Just like the fact we're destroying the rainforests of Brazil (or whatever) isn't even mentioned.

Most of what I call the *deceptional* artists are pretty well aware of that. Really nasty ones, like that ex-Nazi war pilot [snickers]—you know the one that wears a hat all the time... horrid man. Wears a hat; you never see him without his hat... he does things with felt... what is his name? I don't even like to *think* about him so I can't remember his name!

V: Joseph Beuys.

BG: But yeah, one lives in a time when most of the things which *I* value are being destroyed and are disappearing.

V: So when you were doing them you *were* almost in a trance?

BG: Yeah.

V: It must have been amazing; you sat down and—

BG: Well, I didn't just sit down, I *lived* it and *slept* it and *breathed* it for all of those years. I guess I did live in a trance for a great many years.

V: What did some of the Moroccans themselves think about those works? Because their own art isn't representational like that—

BG: No, no... well, they also see the other element—sort of *continuity*. Their own art has a different *space*. All Western art really belongs on a page or on a postcard, no matter what it is. It's a rectangle, whereas there are at least two other principal picture spaces: that of the Chinese and Japanese, which is a folding book—you can't see all of it at one time; it folds and develops as you move it (as I showed you...). Or, it's on a roller and has lengths like an arm's length or a hand's span as being its units—its rhythmic units.

And Arabic art has always been iconoclastic; the idea of *images* was put down about the same time that there were iconoclastic movements in Western society. Byzantine society, for example, went through several revolutions of picture-destroying and statue-smashing, practically simultaneous with the invention of Islam. But the space there is, as they say, "written around the cornices of a room." So to view it, you stand and *YOU* pivot.

V: Hmm...

BG: So one of the basic things that I introduced was **the idea of actually turning the picture space**—which is what that meaning of that text that I wrote for you and drew for you—

V: Turning the picture space?

BG: Yeah. That's that page that I reworked for you. I was interested in all those *basics,* but not within just the framework of Western society. Having lived a more cosmopolitan life than most people, I suppose... you only *see* your own society when you can move out of it and live *outside* it. You look back at it, and you see it in a very different light than you could possibly experience if you lived in it and *nothing but it.* Studying it only from within, you wouldn't understand nearly as much as *one view* of it from the outside would give you. So I left European society, let's say, in 1950, and it might be said, never to have rejoined it completely.

V: Well, the world you depict in those paintings seems

like a much more fraternal, integrated world—less alienated.

BG: Right, yes. My early experience with the Surrealists, who were producing alienation artificially—their principal device was *simulated alienation*—eventually seemed quite *deficient* to me.

V: So much of that was more or less "intellectual conceits"? Would you say it was kind of a *less verbal* society in Tangiers—quite the *opposite* of the Surrealists?

BG: Yes, it's much more integrated. Very few people are alienated from society.

V: Even the *madmen* are kind of integrated!

BG: Yes. [laughs] But the fact is that we've gone through great chronological changes from renaissance time until the present.

In my youth, there were two *poison gases* that were spreading out over the West: Freudianism and Marxism. And they affected everybody—almost everybody got a whiff of those poisons. Other societies have yet to know these disasters.

Take the whole idea of progress: it's unknown in fully integrated societies, and not considered desirable, even. Time stood *still* for twelve or thirteen hundred years for most of Islam, until we burst in upon them and occupied them and conquered them or whatever. And then conquered them even more by our television and blue jeans and emancipation of women and… All those ideas have done much more to destroy their society within the last—well, all the time *I've* known it in—with nothing to replace it. I mean, no *values* to replace it, except *commercial* ones.

But as far as art schools and studying art, the Surrealists were extremely hostile to the whole idea of the Beaux-Arts school; the *established* art. That's one of the reasons (it's not the only reason, but it's *one* of the reasons) that I never had anything to do with them. But then it hadn't turned into *big business* as it has today. I exaggerate, of course, but in my limited way, I thought (when I was twenty) that there were perhaps, oh, fifty painters, of whom five or ten were of some interest. And then there were *groups,* perhaps, in other countries (such as the Bauhaus in Germany or De Stijl in Holland), but those were the only three centers where there seemed to be any organized "art societies," as it were.

Not long ago (given the necessity of having to update one's identity papers, etc), I happened to ask at the prefecture of police how many people were registered as artists. He mumbled sixty. And I went, "Wow, that's a big number!" "Oh no, sixty *thousand!*" he said.

V: Here? In Paris?

BG: Well, in France.

V: Good heavens!

BG: Every *housewife* considers herself an artist, after all! And in America, *migod:* how many more?! When I went to New York in 1940 from war-torn Europe, there were really only *two* galleries that dealt in modern painting. One was Pierre Matisse, who dealt in his father and a couple of other French people, and Julian Levy, who was showing the Surrealists. People like… Betty Parsons was selling books in the Wakefield Bookshop and *illegally* selling pictures in the back of it—the lady who *owned* the bookshop wasn't even supposed to *know* that she was dealing in art. Today, how many galleries are there in New York City?

V: There must be 400...

BG: I believe a good deal more than that! Artists didn't expect to get rich. Whereas today I've heard of some graduates from New York art schools or groups who say, "I'm 25, and I'm not a millionaire yet? Something must be the matter!"

V: "I must be a failure!" [laughter]

BG: Of course, there *were* painters who comfortably operated and made a lot of money like Monet, for example, who always knew he was going to be a rich painter. But nobody believed that their works would ever be seen in the Louvre, for example. Nobody thought that the Impressionists would ever be shown in the Louvre. Certainly, nobody like *Picasso* would *ever* be in there!

So when I saw the Museum of Modern Art in New York—I remember going to a gala opening (must have been in June 1940): it looked to me exactly like Bonwit-Teller's window! I said, "Why, yeah! That's it: modern art has to be modern every week!"

You see the museum across the way here, the Pompidou Centre, has to be brand-new every week. Hectic activity is going on there, employing 1500 people. Dominique Bozot, the head of it, was over here about six months ago and I said to him, "Take a look at your boat from here, take a look at your ship from my window, a boat of which you are the captain." He said, "Yes, and do you know how many people there are in the crew?" I said, "No." He said, "1500." He was thinking of trying to move all of the offices out of the building and into one of the surrounding buildings, but he hasn't been successful so far. But you see what sort of an enterprise it is, and it's already crumbling in front of one's eyes. It's rusting away on the outside—

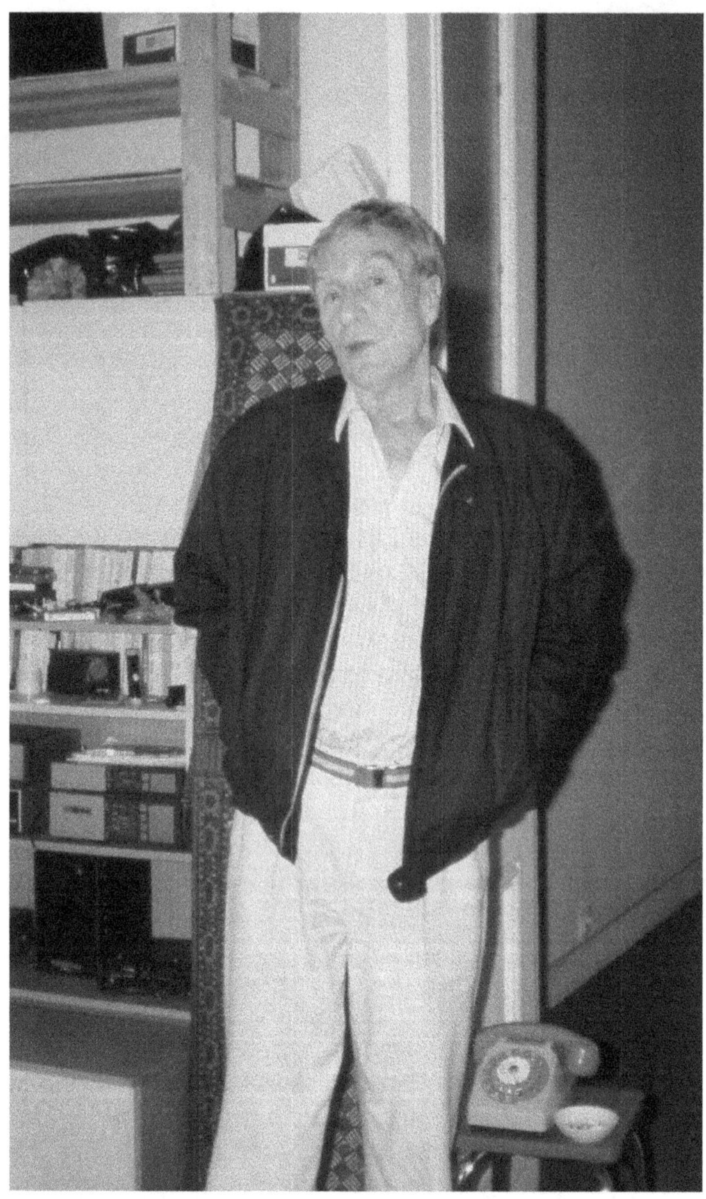

Brion Gysin in his Paris apartment

V: It is?

BG: Well sure, all of those pipes have been proven to be dangerously rusting from inside.

V: Oh, *inside*. There's all that pretty paint covering the outside.

BG: Well, *not* so pretty. Compare my photographs from when it was new to what it is today. Here's a museum that has to be modern every week, and has a new program coming out regularly, announcing *new exciting activities next week, and the week after that.* Museums used to be very *quiet* places for restful, intense intellectual and even psychic experiences. Now there are hordes of tourists being driven through them by dealers with whips!

V: [laughs] So when you first arrived in Morocco *to live,* there was no painting or art there then?

BG: Among Moroccans, you mean? No. Other painters had gone there from the early 1800's; Delacroix had made a famous trip through Morocco, and Matisse had gone there a couple of winters in a row in 1908-11—something like that—and been very influenced by the bright colors and the bright lights. Which of course influenced me, too.

V: Do you mean in the streets and shops?

BG: Yeah, *everywhere*. In a big Matisse show, you will see a lot of Moroccan scenes and women. One of his favorite themes of *obelisks* was picked up there.

V: That's right! I never identified those as being from Morocco. But I haven't liked Matisse since high school...

BG: I was largely responsible for starting many Moroccans painting.

V: Are there other Moroccan painters now?

BG: Oh yes.

V: And they paint on squares and rectangles?

BG: Right.

V: Native Moroccans? What are their names?

BG: Oh, there's, first of all, Hamri, and then there's Yacoubi in London and New York—

V: Oh, he lives in New York. The cook.

BG: No, he wasn't a cook. He was just a boy. Paul Bowles started him out, gave him books by Klee and told him, "That's the sort of thing to do." But it came about by accident, as a matter of fact. He was telling a story in Maghrebi—Moroccan Arabic—like, English Cockneys can't pronounce the letter 'h'; Moroccans in Fez can't pronounce the letter 'k'. So he [Yacoubi] was telling a story about a wild 'at', and Paul said, "What does he mean? What is he talking about?" A very Paul Bowles remark, this; he has to have a precise understanding of anything to understand it at all. So then he said to Yacoubi, "Here's a piece of paper; here's a pencil—draw me this thing!" So he drew this monstrous, very funny thing which was supposed to be a wild *CAT*—a mountain wild cat. That really was a *happy accident* that started *him* off!

[Mohamed] Hamri had painted things for his own amusement. He said, "What do you *call* that?" "Painting." "Oh, I've *always* been doing that!" He would slop colors on the walls and make demons and ladies and jungles—a whole whorehouse section in Rabat was a little, closed *town of prostitution.* And Hamri had spent a joyous season in there, living first in one house and then in the next house, painting the walls, painting all these images—*sinful* ones, in fact—on the walls. [laughs] Sinful because images are considered sinful, especially in a whorehouse. Having a lot of fun with the girls. That's what I wrote in *The Process*, where he brings out his big brush and slaps it on the table: "He's well-endowed with a brush. He had about twelve or fifteen inches of it." [laughter] And then others. There is a "School of Moroccan Painting" now.

V: Hmm. I haven't seen any of this in books.

BG: Yeah, very little has been done about *that*. You mean a book called *Moroccan Painters* or something? I guess it hasn't been done.

V: It hasn't been done—*yet*, at least. *You* could probably do one. You probably know them all.

BG: I do, indeed.

V: Do you think there are more than those two that you just mentioned?

BG: Oh sure, oh yes. There are at least twenty, thirty—maybe fifty interesting ones.

V: So if you returned to Tangiers, you could probably pull together a little project like that?

BG: I wouldn't *dream* of it! Who would it be published by—Abrams Art Books? They wouldn't want to.

V: How many paintings, in that style of the two that are hanging on the wall, have you done? Did you do

others?

BG: You mean how many *hundreds?!?*

V: Hundreds? You did hundreds like those?

BG: Two hundred I sold in America.

V: Like those?

BG: Yes.

V: But each one must have taken days!

BG: It took *years,* but that was how long it took. I mean *time is not purely chronological.* [chuckles] I had shows in New York and Chicago, I forgot, in the fifties (it must be in my *curriculum vitae*) and there were some 220 pictures that I took over at that time, and they all got sold. They were pictures of the desert, emptiness, and pictures of great crowds of people.

V: I love those crowds. Would you say that the reason you had done all these works was just for your own amusement and pleasure?

BG: *Pleasure?* Oh yeah. Yeah, right. Enormous pleasure.

V: I mean, it must be a pleasure to see something like a painting that wasn't there three days ago.

BG: [laughs]

V: Would you say that that was a driving force?

BG: Oh yeah, yeah, yeah, of course.

V: Plus, if you were in a trance making paintings or drawings, then that in itself is an ecstasy.

BG: Yeah, truly. Absolutely, that's the proper word to use.

V: Do you ever feel possessed by another spirit? Or in an elevated state—I hate to use the word "high"?

BG: Well, it's a good word… yeah, sure. Well, when one was, one looked for all of that… one produced a derangement of the senses even, whether through intense application to only one activity … and aided, of course, by lots of grass. The whole world of Morocco, in those days, was a *cloud* of grass smoke… I mean alcohol is forbidden to good Muslims, cannabis was not. Cannabis was sold openly in little markets, where you could go try and test and order ahead… it was a whole different world before people like the American narcotics squad got in there and tried to make a big business out of it—which was their purpose, of course. People had been chewing coca leaves for *thousands of years* before the American narcs got in there and made it into a billion-dollar business.

V: When you say "grass"—

BG: [shouts] CANNABIS!

V: I still find it hard to comprehend a society in which kief smoking and the subsequent states of mind are somehow fully integrated into the society. So music and food and more sensual things are somehow more—

BG: —closely related to it? Yes, of course. Perfectly true.

V: It makes a lot of sense to me. But it's hard for me to comprehend it.

BG: Yes, you think of French food being so tied with wine, German food with beer… there are great divisions, of course, between the grape people and the beer people. In Western society, the beer makers were the barbarians out of the pine woods where the first beers were made with pine buds.

V: Pine buds? As a catalytic agent?

BG: Yeah, yeah, they were fermented and turned into fizzy beer.… get roaring drunk and attack the Romans who were sleeping off their wine.

V: The Romans were sleeping off their wine?

BG: Yeah!

V: What about the kief people?

BG: Well, the kief people managed to put up a whole smokescreen there for over a thousand years. It kept everybody out. The colonials started interfering with that—the French started interfering with that a good deal. [tape recorder turned off]

V: Do you divide up your past by periods?

BG: Not really, no.

V: Would you?

BG: Oh…yeah!

V: How would you, and what would they be called?

BG: I hate to say so, but I suppose the Surrealist period, from 1935-'40.

V: Including the frottages, which were 1942, right? I mean the decalcomania—

BG: Yeah.

V: Then there's the war, of course.

BG: A big hiatus for the war, which was filled in by Japanese studies. I *drew* things at that time—

V: But you didn't save them?

BG: Only one or two... ink and brush drawings, like a hand holding a flower, or something like that. It was a very constructive sort of place where we were, on the campus of the University of British Columbia, on a peninsula called Bray's Point. A great deal of the landscaping on all that part of British Columbia has been done by Japanese gardeners over a period of, oh I don't know, fifty or seventy-five years—now more. Since 1900, at any rate... beautiful gardens—I have photographs of some that still exist.

And that whole area had been very interestingly planted by season, so that flowering trees flowered, and then flowers fell, and there were other colors and other flowers behind in layers—very much like those pictures of Moroccan gardens, which I realized had something of the same idea behind them, creating a visual atmosphere. That influenced me a lot, too, as a matter of fact.

I ceased to do anything strictly representational, like the Surrealist things are, in their distorted way, nevertheless *representational*. Like the drawings are recognizably *anthropomorphic*, I'd say. I became much more interested in nature, and in *soshoro* writing, for example, which is based on the knots and the whole *spring* in bamboo—bamboo painting, it's often called—*translated as.* Where the ink is run, and then the brush stops and creates a knot, and then it goes on…

I became much more aware of the *vital forces in nature.* That's why the little people dance in the crowds, and that's why they look like people; because it's all based on a series of calligraphic signs that are really related to the bamboo sprout as a single seed… it produces a little leg and then comes out and does its whole *life trick.* It has become rich from that on—**that idea of the vital force in the line produced by a brush and running color**… from the attack of the brush on the surface, and the running of the color (whether it's ink or color) producing a *spring*—a lively spring that creates not just a surface glitter, but a *depth of vital force* shown on the canvas.

V: That's very good. It's been said many times that a work of art comes *alive* every time it is viewed by

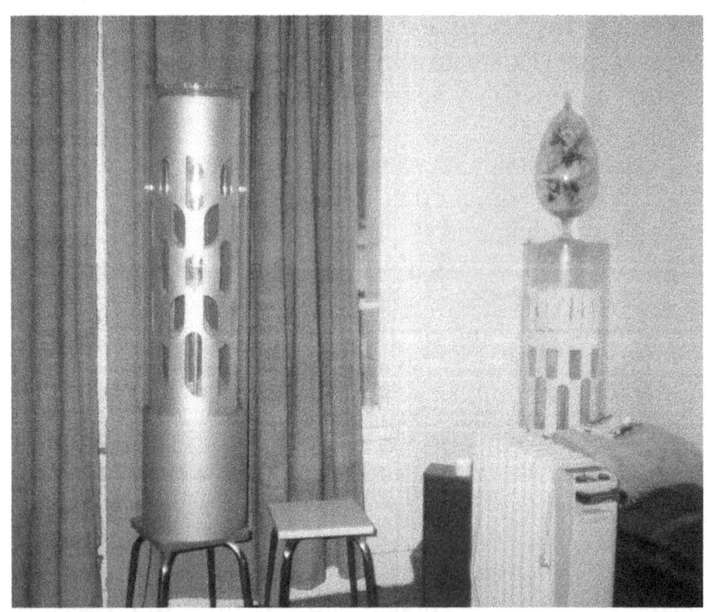

Dream Machines in Gysin's apartment, Paris

someone and their brain works on it.

BG: Right, yeah—

V: It becomes as living as you and I are right now—that work of art is.

BG: Whereas paint laid on by Matisse, or an extreme example De Stijl, laid on with a pallet knife, has nothing of that in it for me at all. It has some kind of interest—it has *historical* interest, or slightly *pictorial* interest—

V: —"pictorial" like a bad photograph—

BG: But it has no sort of *real life force* in it.

V: I agree.

BG: So after the initiation into that by the Japanese master calligraphers that I was acquainted with in Japanese Language School, it has always been present in my work right down to the very latest things that you've seen there—those small (what do I call them?) *capricious cocks,* also have that sort of life in them.

V: You've just given us a kind of *whole new way to look at art again,* as to whether it has that or not!

BG: Yeah, well that's the way I viewed it. So that's why I'm not interested very much in what I call "Deceptual Art".

V: That's not what I *like.* It's a game that you can play and be amused by *following,* but it's not something that actually gives me pleasure—

BG: It may be intellectual, but it's certainly not an emotional—

V: Exactly. I don't feel that pleasure—

BG: I was always looking for that emotional *kick*, as it were—

V: Yeah, that's what I got from that *music;* I got a big kick from that—

BG: Yeah—

V: —and I hadn't felt that for a long time. Actually, that's certainly part of what life's about, is looking for that.

BG: It seems so to me, yeah. It would be nice if we could have that fairly clearly explained in this interview.

V: *That's* what I was after—more. That's very good—that's the *real magic,* because someone like me can sit down and even try to imitate you, but it's gonna take *something else* to get—to transfer that *life force*. You can tell when it's there and when it's not there—

BG: Mmm…

V: Yeah, that's very important.

BG: So that is indeed created in a *state of creation,* which you called "ecstasy" a while ago—very apt. And of course, the awareness of that has become greater since the introduction of the ecstatic drugs to Western society—lots more people have had an experience of that *extra dimension to the world.*

V: They have, but you know, I've tried most of those things myself, as have most people I know,

and almost all of my friends that are the hardest-working people have left it all behind. We've all just left it. I've never quite understood why, but I think it's because we *had* ecstasy and pleasure, but we couldn't *remember* it!

BG: You have to choose between work and play, and in order to get into the *play world* and stay there you have to have a *guide* that takes you into it, and shows you how to use it, or how to carry on with it, and to carry it further. And you can't really then step back from that and go to the office at nine o'clock!

So in that way, I'd say that I have not had discipline; not the *imposed* discipline from the outside. I've imposed a very *expensive* discipline on myself, as it were, through a whole lifetime—most of my lifetime. I've given myself over to a *magic discipline*, if you like, instead of either a *scholastic* discipline of study, or a work discipline of production of a certain kind of... And it's *costly,* very costly, to devote yourself to such researches, such enterprises. There are lots of other things that you *give up,* like happy homes, or regular vacations. [laughs]

And if you get into the *true magic world,* you never *do* come back. Some people go mad, or break it off and give up and do something as revolutionary as *denying* the whole past, as Rimbaud did; he couldn't take any more of it. He went off and sold arms to the natives of Abyssinia!

V: That's the risk; yeah. That's *a* risk—

BG: That's *THE* big risk, yeah, sure enough. But I can't see where to lead into any other subject, except the one of having followed *several* disciplines instead of just one, which would lead one into a sort of Harry Smith-type madness...you know the filmmaker and his little painted images *on and on and on...* that's really somebody who gave himself up to it *entirely,* and there's no exit at all.

Where is he today, I wonder? He's not even in the Chelsea Hotel, is he?

V: I hope he still has his incredible archives.

BG: I wonder.

V: He had one of the best collections of early blues records, like 78s, wax cylinders or whatever.

BG: I never met him, I just know about him; heard about him, but never met… Or at least not that I remember! I may have crossed him in the elevator at the Chelsea, or something.

V: [laughs] So, you were associated with actual Moroccan magicians in Morocco—

BG: Oh yeah, that is what kept me there. I heard them in 1950 at a big feast which is probably pre-Atomic—

V: Actually, I said, "magicians"—

BG: Oh, what?

V: *Magic*.

BG: Yeah, well that's what we're talking about; I mean that exactly. And there was big magic going on because at this particular festival, which occurs in a, presumably, site of Punic origin—Carthagenian—which must have been a grove of sacred prostitute priestesses because of the sexual liberties that were allowed at this feast, still to this day…

First of all, it doesn't coincide with the Islamic calendar but with our calendar because of the *seasons*. Mohammedism—part invented by Mohammed or recaptured by him as a lunar calendar where Christmas occurs in July just as easily as it does in December; the feasts move back eleven days a year to our calendar. So there is a whole other *cycle* going on in Morocco, of obviously more ancient-type magic, to which the *brotherhoods of ecstatic practice* belonged or were drawn in.

I saw something I hadn't ever seen or even read about or heard about: all these different brotherhoods throwing large groups of people (fifty, a hundred people) into *ecstasy*. And out of the corner of my ear, I heard this *other music*. I said to Paul Bowles, with whom I had gone to this festival, that *I wanted to hear this music for the rest of my life.* And Paul went, "Hmmpfh, yeah, well..."

And it took me… 'Cuz I'd gone there meaning to stay a season—if that even—in a little house that Paul also… he said, "You can have the house and stay in it; I'm going to America." Well, he didn't go, actually, at that time. And so, within the year I found these people, by a whole series of happy accidents (as if there *were* any accidents—it must have been *destined,* I think), and they were the musicians of Joujouka. And when I said that I wanted to stay, they said, "Well, sit down then, stay *the rest of your life* here. You're quite welcome."

V: They said this to you? By then you could speak Maghreb?

BG: A little bit, yeah—

V: Enough so they could understand you?

BG: Yeah. So they said, "Well, why don't you go back down to the city and open a little café, and we'll come and make the music, and every night we'll split the take." And instead of being a little café, it was a *palace* that somebody landed me with… and I'm still connected with them to this day, in fact—

V: In touch with—

BG: Well, *more* than in touch; I'm sort of responsible for them—now there's a third generation of them!

V: *Really?*

BG: Yeah... So music has always played a big part in my life. When I look back on the years in New York: the war years and after the war, I think, "How many *painters* did I know? *Not very many.* How many *composers* did I know? Oh, I knew them *all!* How many *writers* did I know? Well... one or two." There's always been a big element of music; as I said at the beginning of this, I can paint happily while listening to music, but when I write I can't *bear*—I mean it's just impossible—

V: Me, too; I can't ever mix the two.

BG: No, a complete distraction. So I don't understand these kids who study with it on—

V: I don't either; it drives me nuts—

BG: Maybe that's why they don't *learn* anything! I don't know. [laughs] Don't learn how to spell...

V: To me, you either listen to music or you talk. I don't even like to have music going in the background when I'm talking with someone; I always shut it off.

BG: Yeah, me too, in principle.

V: In principle. Yeah. If people don't like it, it's just too bad. [Two visitors appear and disappear]

BG: Big goofy men appear that way; it becomes sort of a

pilgrimage that people make here—these kids. So *that* is a sort of contradiction, too: that essentially I should be so *classical* in my way of thinking?! *Conservative* about values?! That I have this reputation of being, among people who are fifty years younger than myself—*migod!* And *they* weren't more than twenty, those two that were just here: earrings in their ears, and rings in their noses, and things. It's an interesting contradiction—or maybe *not* a contradiction; I don't know. But I have the same—or even more—intimate connection with a whole generation of Moroccans that I still see or am in touch with...

V: Moroccan magicians aren't the same as those in the "John Dee School of Western Magic" or the drawing of pentagrams that—

BG: Oh they do; they do indeed.

V: They *do?*

BG: Yeah yeah. I had this wing of a palace, 1001 Nights, where the musicians came and lived and made music—we had marvelous Moroccan food and dancing boys and acrobats and things. But I eventually got into some trouble with some of them and found a—this is a story I've told many a time.

In a ventilator, I found a package. It had obviously a classically, anthropologically-correct package, with seven seeds, seven buds, seven pebbles, seven shards of mirror and then this written material coming together with *god knows what*—menstrual blood and chewing gum and things. And inside was writing which had been written from right to left across the page, and the page turned around—no no, not mirror writing—Arabic; it does go from right to left—and then the page turned halfway and written across so it formed a *grid*. And it was only on seeing *that*, and losing my restaurant over it [laughs], that it seemed to me that I had *neglected* the fact that Arabic written over Japanese produced a grid. And from there came the idea of *turning the picture space*… it came from magic dropped on me in 1955.

V: Didn't you hire a magician to counter that?

BG: I started to get into things like that once, and I saw that that was just *hopeless,* man—you really get yourself into a dreadful mess if you start frequenting magicians. Such a scam: the whole thing.

V: They're not real magicians?

BG: *Of course* they were real magicians! They do real magics and are very important in lots of ways. I mean they deal not only in pentagrams but in poisons. In Islamic society, there are no autopsies, because a verse of the *Qu'ran* says, "Should a man swallow a pearl of great price, his belly may not be opened to find the pearl." So it's quite easy to poison people… an awful lot of poisoning occurs.

V: Good grief, that's horrible!

BG: Well, it just went on—automobile accidents are horrible, too! All sorts of accidents are to be avoided—that's just an accident that is peculiar to that society.

V: You mean poisoning in that society is equivalent to the automobile accident in ours?!

BG: Just about, yeah, and just about as common, too.

V: Jeez, that's funny. Did you ever have a talk with any of these magicians about their disciplines?

BG: Well, they're very shifty people. What do you mean? They're not going to be giving away their trade secrets that easily. But in *The Process* I wrote about a magician who got into the house and produced what in effect was a *chasm* opening in the room; apparently he fell into it himself!

V: Right.

BG: But... magic is a very dirty business, to be avoided if possible. In *our* society it led to being burnt at the stake after all, didn't it? And a few philosophers went up in flames, like Giordano Bruno and a couple of others. Even Pico de la Mirandola just *escaped.* I don't know; it's a dirty business, and it doesn't pay off to be interested in magic too closely. And if you *hire* magicians, you're in *their grasp*—not them in yours. Do you think they're in our pay? No no, we were in their hands!

V: It's probably best to leave them in their own world—

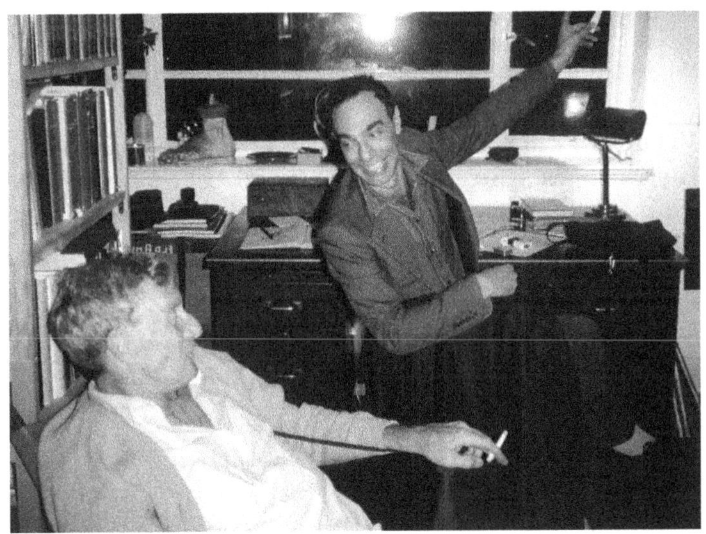

Brion Gysin visiting Derek Jarman

BG: Um, absolutely. But anybody who has lived in those countries for a long time has always had something to do with them…

V: I had this album that Paul Bowles wrote the liner notes for, titled *Jilala*—that green-and-black album—

BG: Put out by Ira Cohen?

V: I don't know who put it out—maybe.

BG: I recorded one side, and Paul recorded the other?

V: It's been a long time since I've seen it. It describes things like how in ecstasies people could swallow kettles of boiling water and slash themselves with knives and all these things, and then after it's over apparently there are no ill effects.

BG: Well, aren't they studying that at Stanford University? Aren't people walking through red hot coals every day of the week now in Southern California?

V: I didn't know about that… SRI [Stanford Research Institute] is studying that? I mean that's obviously kind of "magical"… and you *saw* things like that happen—

BG: Oh yeah, sure!

V: And you were amazed, right?

BG: Well no, no—not amazed. [laughs]

V: Really?

BG: Well, no. I knew about it, read about it, or was associated with people who either practiced it or knew a good deal about it, or who were capable themselves of hiring magicians, or even using it against one—like, "Who put that in my ventilator?" That was only one case; there were several others. I always expressed a rather... righteous disapproval of all of that. *Save yourself*—that's a word to the wise, I think. But yeah, magic—cures and things like that—have gone on a long time.

V: Well, you're a magician in a different way then, because you have found an ability to transmute *life force* onto paper—

BG: That's what I figured, yeah.

V: —using inks, paints, watercolors. I think that's really good.

BG: That seemed to be the only thing to *do*... if one were as deeply wrapped up in it as I was: plunged into it and still anxious to *survive*. One had to *use* it in one's *own* way. So I first found out—I remember shortly after that—from *doing* some of these magic writings, which *horrified* Moroccan friends who saw them—

V: Why?

BG: Because naturally, everybody is afraid of it—of the dangers involved. And then they would look a little bit closer and say, "Wah wah yeah, wah wah yeah—little people are dancing right across the page!"

V: Hmm.

BG: They came right out of the ink pot?! [laughs] And that's why they dance in those pictures of crowds, is because they use those techniques to make 'em do so... *while looking away!*

V: "While looking away"?

BG: Look away! The Occident is always trying to look *closer,* like down a microscope or something like that... whereas **the Oriental way is to *learn how to look away.***

V: Really?

BG: Mmm... LOOK AWAY! As I said much earlier, about seeing Max Ernst's *frottage*, there's a way of making the painting *make itself.* I recognized the connection; some of his *frottages* are quite *magical* in a way in that owls appear out of the *frottage* of the boards of the floor or whatever, so that one recognizes in veneers on furniture, for example, in a place that's frequented by lots of artists all the time... in a place on the river down here where there's probably 150 studios. The elevators are *filled* with a veneer which is on the inside of the elevators if you point it out to people... it's *filled* with little magical faces grimacing and dancing and thumbing their noses at you.

V: Just in the wood, itself?

BG: Yeah. So the answer to *that* is that *they're living in a different time.* They're *alive,* and if you ruin them in an elevator I don't know *what* you've done to them!

They're developing by your vision of them—your vision of them brings them back into a sort of life—but you realize this has nothing whatever to do with a *clock*—it has to do with a completely different sort of clock—a *different time.* So magic really is a *parallel world* existing in *another time* than the one that you and I are breathing in, and me smoking and drinking in, at this moment.

V: That must be very strange to have these cyclical festivals which every year are eleven days earlier, so that you do end up with a Christmas in July. I just can't imagine the effects. You must have experienced it; can you kind of explain what it must have felt like? That must be very strange—

BG: Well, it makes life much more *exciting!*

V: Oh yeah, of course!

BG: Much more interesting than dumb old Santa Claus coming, and his stupid old reindeers, at snow time—

V: Okay. The first festival you went to was a fertility festival, right?

BG: Yeah, it had to do with harvests, obviously.

V: What are some of the other kinds?

BG: Well, the other kinds are the ones that are connected with the Islamic calendar. So people like the musicians of Joujouka, because they are presumably a *Pagan survival,* have been forced by circumstance—

V: —back to Lupercalia—

BG: In order to survive, they've attached themselves to the principal feast in the Islamic year which does move back through time. I mean, this summer the feast will occur in late May or early June, where... It takes 32 years to come back to the same time.

V: By our calendar—

BG: —by our calendar, yeah, and our calendar being

correct seasonally... because of, you know, our slight adjustment of Leap Year and all that. But ours is essentially the Julian calendar which already existed at the time of Mohammed. The Roman calendar was more correct than theirs is, but he made the conscious choice of the lunar calendar. He must have been a very, very smart cat—very, very smart—'cuz he realized that this would make it more exciting and more fun and more *intense*.

And of course the month of fasting by day and feasting by night—which is more sensible than our Lent was—our Lent always fell in the part of the year when nothing was growing, and so people actually fell into terrible states of scurvy and malnutrition during the Christian Lent.

V: Huh...

BG: But this can occur sometimes—when it occurs in midsummer, as it did the first years that I went there—naturally it's an enormous sacrifice because the night is so short. The sun sets at 9:15, for example, and the sun rises at 2:15, so you've got only those few hours to eat in, and you've got these tremendously hot days you can't drink a single drop of water—eat nothing, smoke nothing, etc. So it produces a *cyclical* event, which, until the time of industrialization and modern government, etc, where people are now—it's *demanded* of them to work during this month, or to open the government offices—which they used not to do. When the month of fast fell in the summertime, everything used to close down. Now it doesn't anymore, so there are also *backsliders* and *secret eaters!* The whole thing's kind of *falling apart.* [laughter]

But, as I said, to live completely and *for so long* outside of one's own society in which one had been born gives one an enormously perceptive view of one's own thing, while learning another and living with another. You look back on it and you say, "Woo—this looks altogether different."

You're living all your life in it. You see that you were so involved that you *cannot* see really what's going on.

V: Yeah, right down to the very calendar with its built-in feasts and celebrations.

BG: Right.

V: That you never question, *normally*—

BG: Right.

V: I've always hated most of the holidays; the only one I like is Halloween.

BG: Halloween?!? [laughs]

V: I think there should be *more* Halloweens!

BG: Uh huh.

V: I mean, more opportunities to put on masks; things like that.

BG: No, there are very few places except—*Venice* is the one where there's a *long* carnival that lasts a whole month with people in disguise down the street.

V: What month?

BG: Well, *now*—it's just now over.

V: I just missed it! I want to go sometime. Have you ever gone to that?

BG: No, let's see… I was there at Christmas time, and it began. Everybody was already *preparing* for it, and friends with whom I was staying were having their masks made and were refurbishing their costumes. Actually, I was so ignorant of it that I thought it lasted only a day or two. I didn't realize that for the *whole month* it was going on.

V: I didn't know that either; that's amazing. I *have* to go there during that month.

BG: Hmm, yeah. It's very exciting 'cuz it's also the time that you're gonna have the high water and the Piazza San Marco and half of the whole city is flooded. You have to walk around on wooden pontoons, and there are no tourists and the whole city is turned in on itself!

V: Huh—it's not a tourist time?

BG: No.

V: But I could visit; *you* could visit if you wanted...

BG: Oh yeah. But most tourists don't. They're not encouraged, and they don't know about it, and when they get there they find it very uncomfortable!

V: Hmm...

BG: —a little bit creepy, and then there's all this water everywhere! [laughs]

V: Well, Brion, I'm impressed that you've gotten this full experience in a society that may be more integrated. But you can't do that anymore—this is why I'm interested in hearing about it. You have an understanding of a society which seems much less dependent on intellectual tricks and verbiage.

BG: Uh hmm...

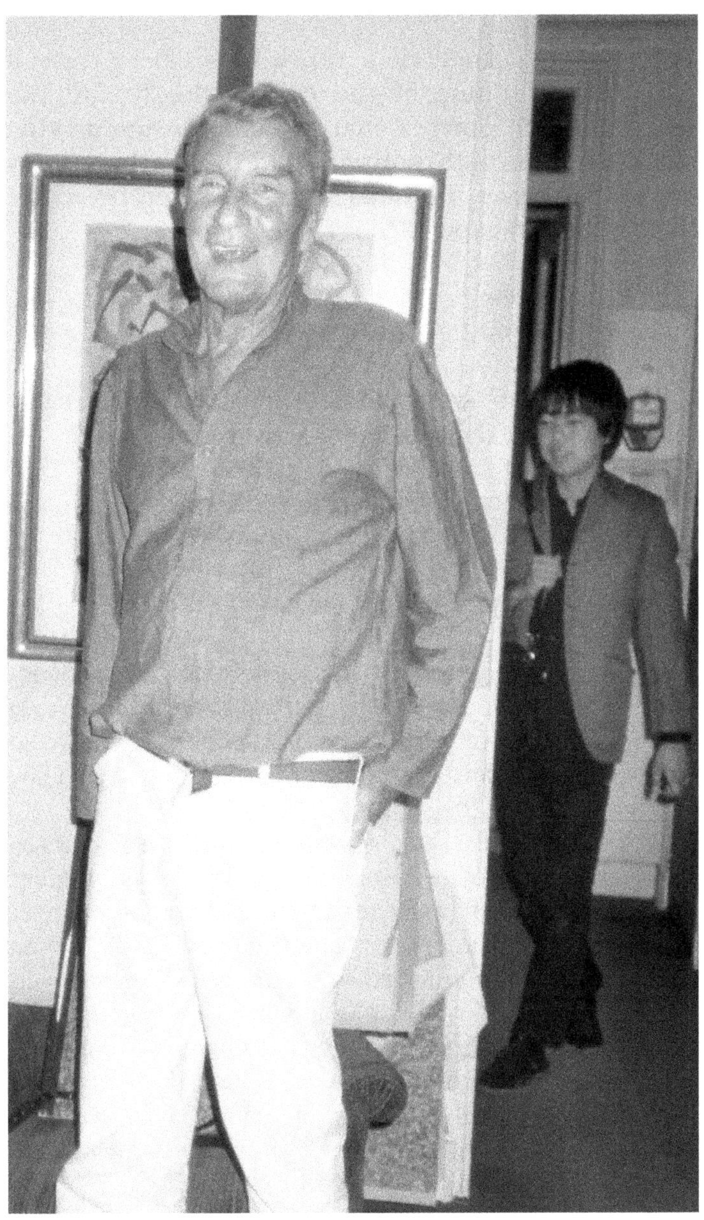

Brion Gysin and V. Vale in Paris

V: Yet at the same time you also seem to have a real understanding of the *rest* of the world: the real economic powers that be and the underlying machinations, both political and other, that go on *behind* the news. I glimpsed the way you interpret the daily newspaper—

BG: Yeah, [laughs] true. I don't *read it and believe it*—no. I take its temperature every day! Yeah.

V: How do you know about the way things really work; the way these decisions are really made?

BG: Well, I've met a lot of people within the *power circuit* as it were—well, not a *lot,* but certainly enough to—

V: More than most people meet—

BG: Yeah. When I was young, around twenty, I saw a lot of the people who had just recently *lost* power by World War I. I saw a lot of people who had been ruined but who had understood perfectly some of the big players… They lost that round of the *game*.

And then also the advantage (and disadvantage, really, in a big way, too) of having gone to *the* number one Catholic school (and the Catholics being out of power since the Reformation—in England, certainly). By an education being connected with the group of *losers* in English society! It wasn't until I was just about ready to graduate that I realized that nobody from our school could ever *get* to a position of power, although that was what we were presumably being trained for! There were no Catholics in the foreign service, for example in England, or no Catholics in government in England.

V: No MPs?

BG: A few maybe; a couple of Liberal [political party] MPs. And then the Irish being completely put out of it for—god knows—forever. Maggie Thatcher goes all the way to Washington to tell Reagan to forget that he's Irish and to have nothing whatsoever to do with those Irish—

V: Really?

BG: Sure, that was one of her big messages when she went.

V: Good grief—

BG: She wanted to see to it that no Irish money got to the I.R.A. and such.

V: Because they had been sending money over?

BG: Oh yeah, yeah. An insane situation. Well, I don't feel overprivileged tonight, I admit.

V: Why?

BG: Why should I feel overprivileged? I am *not*. I'm running down.

V: Brion, you gotta tell me once more this incredible story of how you almost found the Holy Grail—

BG: Oh yeah—

V: And how that even came about—

[suddenly the tape ends]

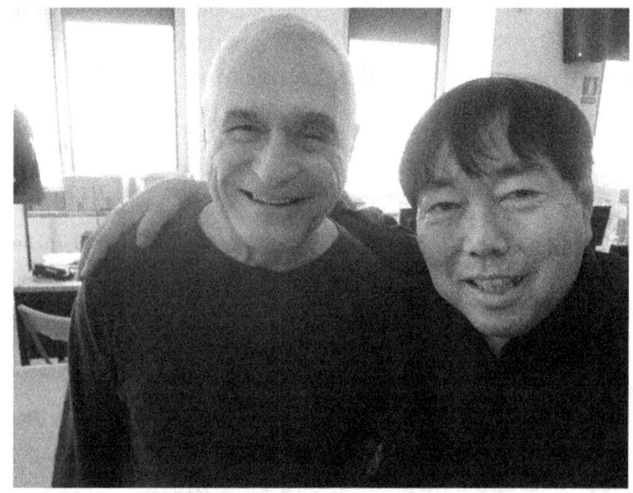

John Giorno and V. Vale in Barcelona, Spain

JOHN GIORNO: Doing the Third Mind

Poet and performance artist John Giorno (born December 4, 1936) met William S. Burroughs and Brion Gysin in the '60s and formed close relationships with both. In this previously unpublished interview from July 1986, recorded during a visit to the RE/Search office in San Francisco, Giorno discusses his career as well as his time spent with Burroughs and Gysin while they were collaborating on The Third Mind. *He also talks about spending time with Andy Warhol.*

John Giorno: Did you get both those cats as kittens?

V. Vale: Well, first there was Mr. Cat. Then Mr. Cat had kittens—more or less. But he seemed to recognize that this one kitten was his "son". [laughs] They got along okay, and then we got this girl cat. Then the son kind of got an Oedipal complex and started attacking Mr. Cat all the time for no reason. So Mr. Cat and the girl cat are like good friends. I don't know if you have any cats.

No, but I have guest cats and friends who have cats, so—they're *enough!* [laughs] Like, there's a great Russian Blue in the building which comes and visits William and me, and it stays for the night (or two nights) and then goes. And whenever it's nine o'clock at night, and I'm ready to start a *certain kind of work*—I get drunk and stoned and I'm *really going*—well *that's* the time it decides to wake up and, you know, *do that thing*. It constantly takes you away from whatever you're doing when it's *important*. When it's ***NOT*** important they couldn't care less!

Yeah—I think they sense your level of metabolic activity. When *you're* sleeping, *they* sleep. When you get active, they get active.

It was great seeing that guy last night—

Mark McCloud [curator of the LSD Museum in San Francisco]. Like I said, he's one of the few people I like in San Francisco. I always learn something every time I go over there, and definitely have fun, so I guess he's worthwhile on both counts.

If he doesn't come tomorrow, I'll get his address or something. It's not very good grass but the fact that he gave such a great bag is—

He's a really sweet guy. Kind of a generous guy, I

guess—that's just the way he is. He moved all of my furniture in here a long time ago with his truck—he sort of rescued me out of a situation. We had a really good party at his place *years* ago at his studio on 17th Street.

Was that the William Burroughs birthday party, for the record?

It was one of them, yeah. [RE/Search and Survival Research Labs hosted two birthday parties for Burroughs in 1982 and 1983.]

I went to one of those. There was a great party in a loft for *Nothing Here Now But The Recordings*.

Was it the time we showed slides of tattooed people?

That might have been the one—

Ed Hardy, who's like the best tattoo artist in the world, helped the party out by showing huge slide displays of some of his tattoos. And then there were video monitors set out with SRL war games on—so if it was *that* one, you were there! That was at Mark McCloud's former studio before he bought that house on 20th Street.

I have to admit that my thoughts have been around Brion Gysin for the last week or so. It was pretty touching what you said last night about how *before* he got the fatal diagnosis, he grabbed you and said—

It was quite moving—it was one of the most moving things I've ever seen from Brion, because he *dug* his fingers in my hand and was *completely shaking:* "Uh-uh-uh-uh-uh-uh-uh I'm *afraid* to die, I'm *afraid* to die, I'm afraid to stay alive! What'll I happen if I stay alive? [high pitch] Uh..." Finally, I was going to leave but didn't—this was at the end of three or four hours... It was at the end of a great day, actually! [laughs]

That's like the "moment of truth" or something—

It was very peaceful, being in the room with him and his corpse, you know? One didn't get any kind of a freaked-out feeling—that he was freaked out, or disturbed, because you sensed that he was definitely *there.* You felt he was very *peaceful*... in the darkness.

You've been to Paris?

I've been to his apartment several times—

They had the windows closed. Every time I went in they'd close the door behind me and Fafa [François de Palaminy] would let in just *this much* of the morning light—the *dark* morning light! [laughs] And he was cremated today, actually.

I woke up and thought, "This is the moment he's being cremated," but he was really already *gone!* [laughs]

Oh, well. Maybe you'll make it to that south coast of Morocco for that memorial—

No, that's not *my* job—that's going to be Fafa and John O'Neill.

Oh, *they're* going to do that. Actually, I heard that a lot of his friends were supposed to gather on that south coast for the dispersal of Brion's ashes—

At one point it was supposed to be Felicity Mason, but Felicity didn't want to do it *herself*, and she was making some plan that she and William would go to *Joujouka* rather than the coast. Maybe they'll go soon?

Tell me everything you can about Brion. I'm amazed that, off the record, you've known him about twenty-one years—around 1965 you took acid with him in the Chelsea Hotel—

Not "off the record" if you want to actually print it! I met him in '64 when he and William arrived in November or December. And it was *the big trip* because William hadn't been back for like ten or twenty years—it was his "Return to America." And Brion, he'd left right after World War II, so I guess it was twenty years. This was sort of a *triumphant return* because William was really famous, so they had come to "make the deals."

William did this reading at 222 Bowery, on the top floor. This friend of mine, Wynn Chamberlain, who's a painter—he had the top floor. He gave these great parties and *whatnot,* and he got this idea that *William should do a reading.* And Mack Thomas, the novelist who lives in New Mexico—he was published by Grove, and William was published by Grove, so he got both of them to read. I think this was March of '65: they had a reading and *everyone* came. There was a big article about it in the *New York Times*—we had Avedon there, and Diana Vreeland, and more of the "Pop" people—well, this was '65 and Andy Warhol and Robert Indiana and Claes Oldenburg and *whatnot* were just "the Pop artists"—they hadn't become famous yet. It seemed like this was William's first public reading.

And this was on the top floor of 222 Bowery where you met him?

Well, there were these various parties. Panna Grady gave parties and there William did *another* reading. Diane di Prima had something on February 14, Valentine's

Day, in a small theater on Fourth Street on a Sunday afternoon. Brion did a little something—I can't remember *what* happened, and lots of other people did something. Anyway, *there were all these events.* By then I was *living* with Brion in the Chelsea—

—sort of like a "close relationship"?

Yeah, taking my *very first* acid trip, which was followed by thirty-one others [laughs] into the spring and the summer—in the non-air-conditioned Hotel Chelsea, *sweating* through these incredibly long, really *heavy* acid trips. Your first acid trips are your most important. Brion was just sort of a great guy—that's why I'm so *indebted* to Brion.

I mean I've had lots of problems with Brion over the years, as we all have: all of the bad things that he says about you, and then he gets sort of angry, and it gets worse, and then you all come together and forget about it... and it gets worse *again!*

That was '65. Then I went to Morocco in February of '66.

Where did you *get* LSD? In 1965 it wasn't really that well-known—

From this guy Stanley Angles [sic] in New York. He knew Brion (and he's still around; he was a dealer). It was sugar cubes. You buy them from Stanley and go home quickly and put them in the refrigerator, because if you didn't it would just evaporate! This was early LSD that didn't *stick;* after a few days it sort of lost it.

Even in the fridge?

If you kept it in the freezer it would *sort of* keep for a while. But if you just left it out, it would vanish. *No no no,* the *very* first acid I bought was from Ira Cohen who lived on Norfolk Street. After a while, there were so many trips that Stanley Angles was who we scored from.

Thirty-two trips! Were they all in your room in the Chelsea? What was the room number?

703. If not 703, it was 704 or 705.

So at the time you were a young poet and an avant-garde guy—

I was just this kid who came from—

Oh, you were this cute kid! You hadn't always lived in New York?

I was *born* in New York; I was always there.

But you were *advanced*. So no wonder you could score—you were already "hip", so to speak.

Due to whatever luck. *Sleep* [a famously-long Andy Warhol film of John Giorno sleeping] had been made in '62 or '63.

That's right! I saw that movie *ages* ago, and didn't know it was *you* in it. How did *that* happen? Were you just the right guy at the right place... what happened?

In those years—'62 through '65—I saw Andy all the time. Andy sort of *picks up a person.* I met Andy through Wynn—actually, I went to his opening and it wasn't even the Marilyns, it was the one that had the soup cans—

The one that had the daisies?

No, that was later. I think the opening had the soup cans and maybe the gold Marilyn… but it had the earlier pictures—he drew these things which *weren't that great* (and the Troy Donahue and whatever). Then shortly afterward Wynn had the three of us over for dinner down at 222 Bowery. Back then I used to sleep all the time. Andy would call at four in the afternoon—I'd be asleep… ten in the morning, I'd be asleep [laughs]… He'd say, "What are you *doing?*" I'd say, "I'm asleep." We'd be meeting at six o'clock to go to those things which one never does anymore—there was *always* an opening; it was the Pop Artists—

So what was "happening" were openings?

Openings that everyone went to. Because at the time Claes Oldenburg or Roy Lichtenstein—nobody was famous. It was their *first shows* that everyone went to. And there were all these parties that everyone went to because the parties were connected to these twenty-four people.

A lot of times we went to see all the Jonas Mekas and the Cinemathéque (or whatever it was called) screenings [Filmmaker's Cinemathéque, which later evolved into Anthology Film Archives]. One day we were watching—actually, we were *leaving;* we had seen Ron Rice and Jack Smith's *Flaming Creatures* for the third time, and ten other of these films, and they were awful! Andy said [imitates Warhol's voice]: "They're so awful! Why doesn't somebody make a beautiful movie—there's so many *beautiful* things!" A few weeks later he bought a camera, a Bolex, and he got the idea to do *Sleep* 'cuz I was sleeping all the time—

That was one of his first films, the one with you?

It was his *very first.*

Wow!

And actually *how* it happened, how he got the idea, is: we went to Wynn Chamberlain's rented place in the country, up in Old Lyme, Connecticut, where Eleanor Ward [art dealer and founder of the Stable Gallery in New York] had this farm. There were two houses: Eleanor had one of the houses and Wynn had the other. Andy and I went up for a weekend with Marisol [Escobar], I think—

Wow!

—and we drank tons—it was hot, it was summertime—we drank tons of (besides the wine and everything) Demerara rum—that sort of 150-proof rum. It was hot and of course I went to *SLEEP.* I was *so* drunk, but it was one of those things where I was sleeping with one eye open. Every once in a while I'd look over and Andy was on speed during those years, you know—

Really?

Well, it was the years that he was on speed, and he'd be awake sort of propped up *looking at me!* And I'd just fall back asleep… You know how it is when you're drunk: two hours later you wake up to take a piss, and I'd say, "What are you *DOING?!*" And he'd say, "I'm watching you!" [laughs] I'd fall back, or take a piss or whatever it would be, and then it was shortly after that—a day or two—he got the idea to make a movie about sleep.

It was an *eight-hour* film, wasn't it? [5 hours and 21 minutes] They showed it ages ago in Berkeley on Shattuck Avenue. It ran all night, and you had the option of coming and going. You said that Warhol

had the tendency to meet somebody and—

He'd sort of fall in love with you for a while and start using you—like he did with all those who later became the Superstars—with Edie and on and on and on... You thought it would last forever, but it would only last two or three years. Suddenly you'd be "out"! [laughs]

Would he just not return your phone calls?

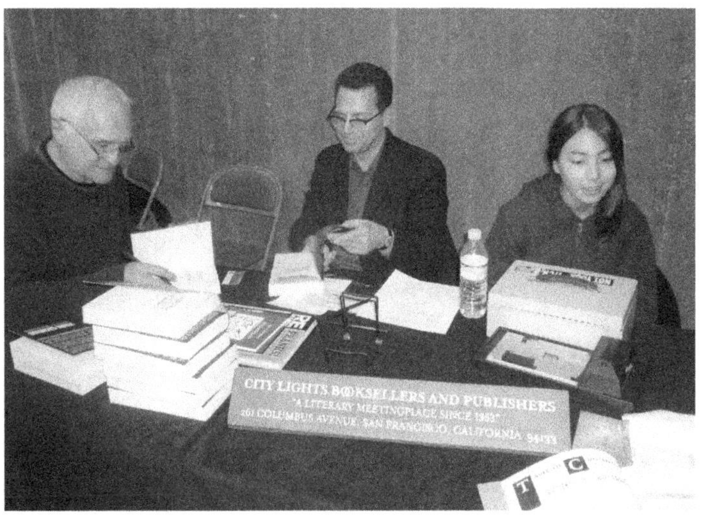

John Giorno and friends, City Lights book release event, San Francisco

Exactly.

And suddenly you were "shut out" or something?

The scene would *change,* you know. Like the early years of Naomi Levine and me and Gerard Malanga—Gerard was *working* there, so Gerard had this thing that was *sustained* because he was working with the actors and sweeping the floor—in the early years he'd *just run errands.* Like in *Sleep*, he brought the rolls of film to be developed and

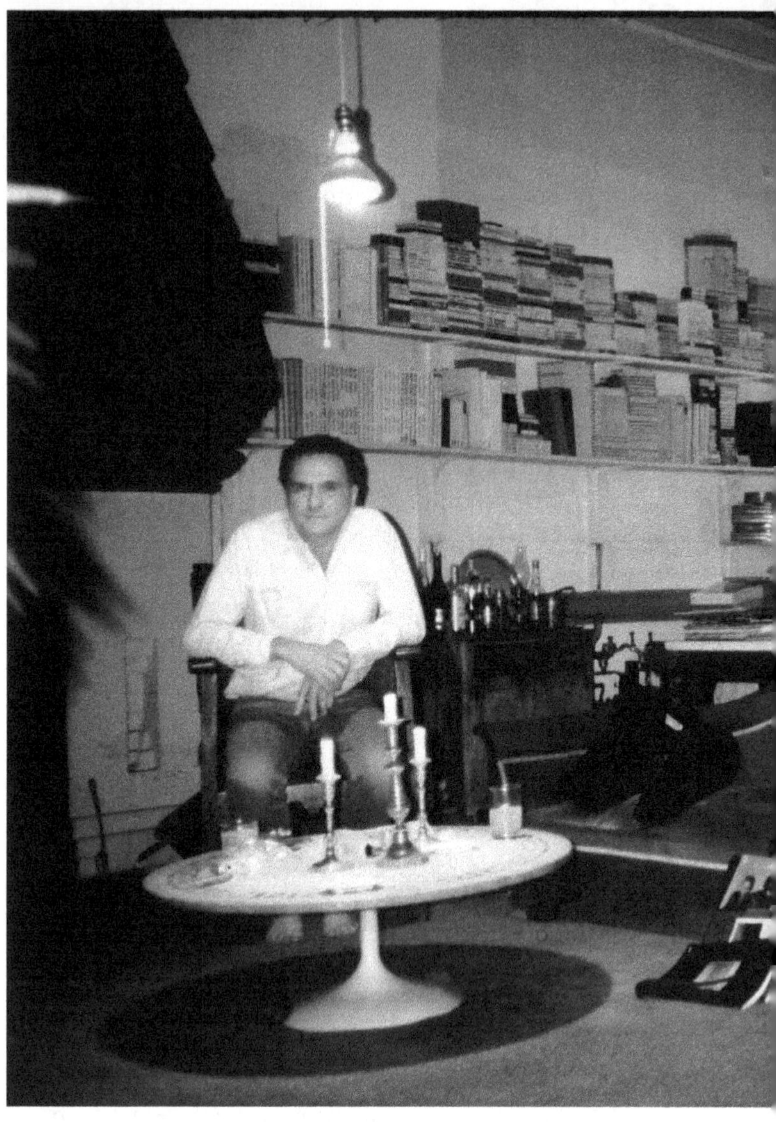

picked them up three days later. Gerard was going to school at Wagner College in Staten Island. He was Andy's new college assistant or "intern".

So Warhol sort of *protégéd* you for a while?

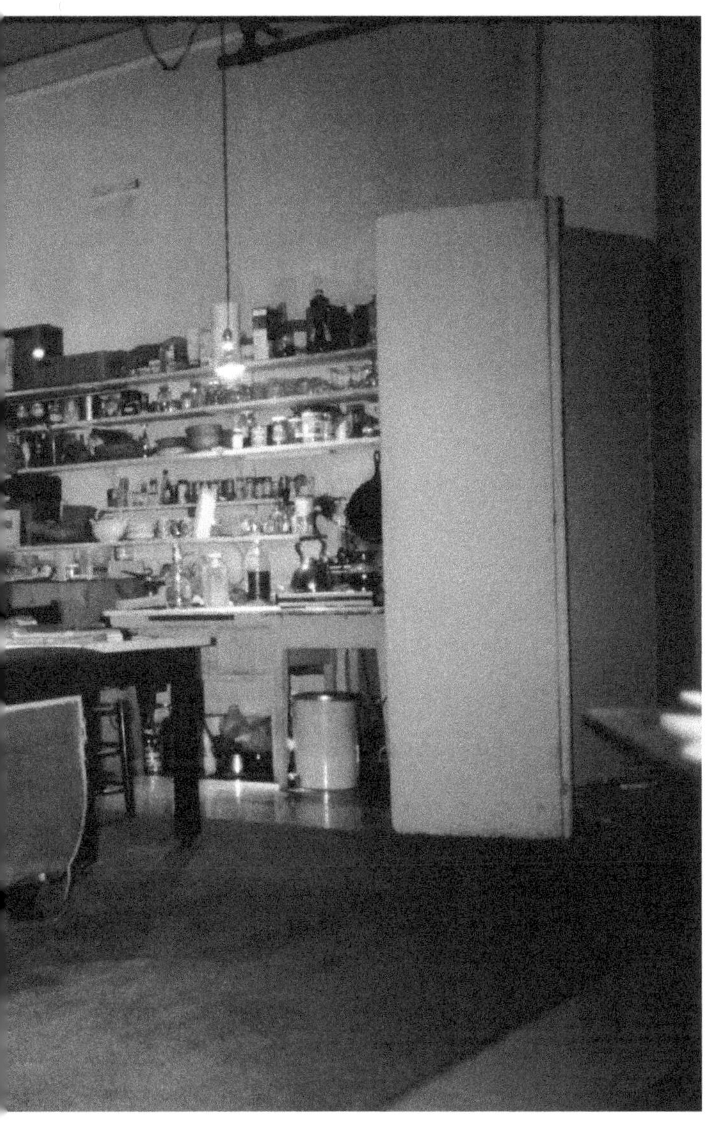

John Giorno at The Bunker, NYC

Uh-huh.

He took you out to dinners and things like that?

No, it was just *going to something every night.* Literally, there was an opening or a party amongst all of them *every night.*

That sounds really exciting—

It *was* exciting but it wasn't fun! Everyone was so *fucked-up,* you know? Everyone was taking a lot of speed, or drinking—this was before LSD: '62 and '63 and '64. So nobody knew how to *deal* with him. Maybe later you became more *aware* of your mind and what was going on in it so you could deal with it better. But those glamorous years of the early 1960s were *totally* fucked up! [laughs] I and everyone else were *totally* unhappy in a *completely intense* way.

All that speed?

Uh-huh.

Still, it seems like Warhol got a helluva lot of work done—he cranked out a lot of films—

Those were his only years, really, for creating *a lot.*

That's actually my favorite period: those intense paintings of the electric chair and car crashes and airplane crashes—

Before he became famous or acknowledged, Andy was *constantly* being cut down by everyone. The generation before was Rauschenberg and Jasper Johns and de Kooning and those people completely hated Andy and were *ruthlessly* cruel to him.

In person?

In person or—you know how *bitchy* everyone is, in

whatever they would say and do. So Andy was completely tortured in *his* own way during those years, of being *hurt all the time*—just being humiliated or hurt. Bob or Jasper or whoever would say a thing or two because they had known him from *before* when he was a shoe—designed or drew those shoes, or did Bonwit-Teller windows, or advertisements, or whatever it was.

Ah, he was stigmatized for being a "commercial artist"! What was it like being around Warhol? Did he talk and discourse and philosophize and give theory, or was he not talkative at all? What's he *LIKE* to be around?

In those years he talked about what he was doing. Actually, it was more like: he wasn't *telling* me what he was doing, but—you know the way people talk to

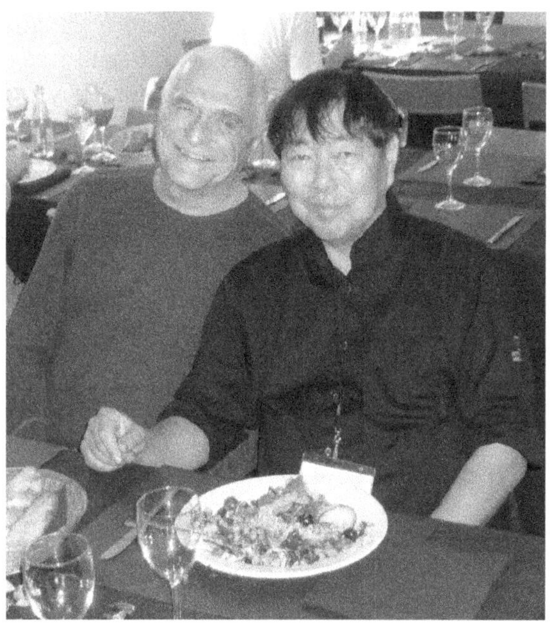

John Giorno and V. Vale

themselves about what they're feeling, or why he liked Marilyn, or *why* he liked something. It was like feeling somebody working.

Wow! You could *learn* from that—

That's how I started. It was through Andy that I started doing *found images,* because at that time I was a *poet.* Lord knows what I was writing—I'm sure it's as bad as it could possibly be! I think I *stopped writing* because I was busy—

You had some *living* to do—

That was the time of John Ashbery and Frank O'Hara, and even though Frank was a really big influence on me, it just seemed to be incredibly boring! I did one of those things like, "There's so many beautiful words—why doesn't somebody write a *beautiful* poem?" [laughs] I did what Andy did. I mean, Andy sort of found images and would then *make* a Campbell's soup can or Troy Donahue or Marilyn *whatever.* I took that!

One day I was reading the *New York Times* and saw that Freddie Herko had committed suicide. It was his obituary that so moved me—maybe just one or two sentences—and I made that into a *poem* by drawing slashes where the pauses in my mind were. So it was through *Andy* that I got to that idea—

—of being alert for found images.

Or found poems that didn't come from any *literary* source.

And you borrowed an "art idea"—

It wasn't from Dada or people who used found images in the 20s, 30s and 40s—it came to me though *Andy.*

He gave you the *idea*. The thing I've always liked about Warhol is how unaffected and natural and direct his responses seem to be... to just what's obviously *there*. It must have been amazing to be there when he's kind of "developing his theories"—

It helped because it was incredibly difficult! Because when I started developing the single-found-image and making short poems (the *American Book of the Dead)*, there was a little group of Ted Berrigans who also got the idea [laughs]... Ted Berrigan was another sort of person who totally *helped*. When somebody likes what you're doing, it's a great blast of energy that makes you feel good and want to do more. There was Ted and a couple of other people in that Lower East Side poetry scene that sort of encouraged one another.

But not you?

I was a poet and everyone hated me just as much as they hated Andy, but Andy at least had the art world. But I was just this "pathetic poet" and it was really difficult until I met Brion. Brion saw it instantly, and William saw it instantly.

What did they see?

They saw the *clarity* and sparkle or energy in what I was doing—and I was *encouraged*. One was with Brion and with William while they were "doing the *third mind*" and just picking up all the information *subliminally*—there was all kinds of it—from what *they* were doing, which made it presumably grow.

Oh, yeah—just the way William reads the newspapers, just learning from that alone. How alert he was to these weird news items on page 43

which are more significant than the articles on page one—just that alone.

The biggest influence on me was actually *The Job,* not *Naked Lunch.* I practically *memorized* those interviews that came out. There was a big excerpt in *Evergreen Review* before the book came out and I was amazed by that…

Good! So those guys immediately took *you* under their wing, so to speak.

And then Brion did something else for me, which was: introduce me to technology. Even though "technology" was at the time just a little tape recorder!

They weren't common then.

Then we did a poem—a collaboration. He did the sound part; we went around the subway collecting found subway sounds—the trains rolling, and… We felt *so important!* [laughs] This $60 tape recorder was *big* (not like now)—a portable clunker the size of a typewriter. We borrowed other tape recorders and made overlays and did this poem called "Subway Poem"… I sent it to Paris to be included in the Paris Biennale.

The *Poetique Domaine*—you know, [François] Dufrêne, and [Bernard] Heidsieck and [Henri] Chopin and Brion—which was the "*poésie sonore*" happening—

Right, that "sound poetry" thing.

And it's through *that*—fiddling around that one summer with tape recorders—that started me on this long career of twenty years—well, I stopped doing that about five years ago.

You stopped using that Walkman with echo/delay—

No, I stopped doing the found poems *more* than five years ago—more like six or seven or eight years ago—and I stopped doing that kind of permutation back in '81 or…

God, it was that long ago! I'm glad I got to see that.

But that's why I'm so indebted to Brion, because he was responsible for my whole life, really—that enormous period of time from [the sixties to the eighties]…

That must have been incredible to be there when nobody else was doing it, when there was no theory in print about doing that... You knew you were *on to something*.

So Brion and William had this working relationship with you, and you got to observe them at work. Did you learn anything else from Brion—like the *way* he worked? Would he, as soon as he got up in the morning, do something?

They essentially had an idea that they were working nine to five.

"The Job"! [laughs]

Brion and I wouldn't wake up until ten o'clock, and then it would be, "I'm late!" [laughs] We had these horrible hangovers, just managing to get a cup of coffee... He'd go down to Center Street, where William had a loft at that time above where the Atomic Machinery Exchange [sic] was, and they'd work all day until five.

Would he be at a desk or a typewriter?

At a desk. It was a loft, so there were these tables and typewriters. William, then as now, likes to stop at five o'clock and have a drink. That's the end of the work day!

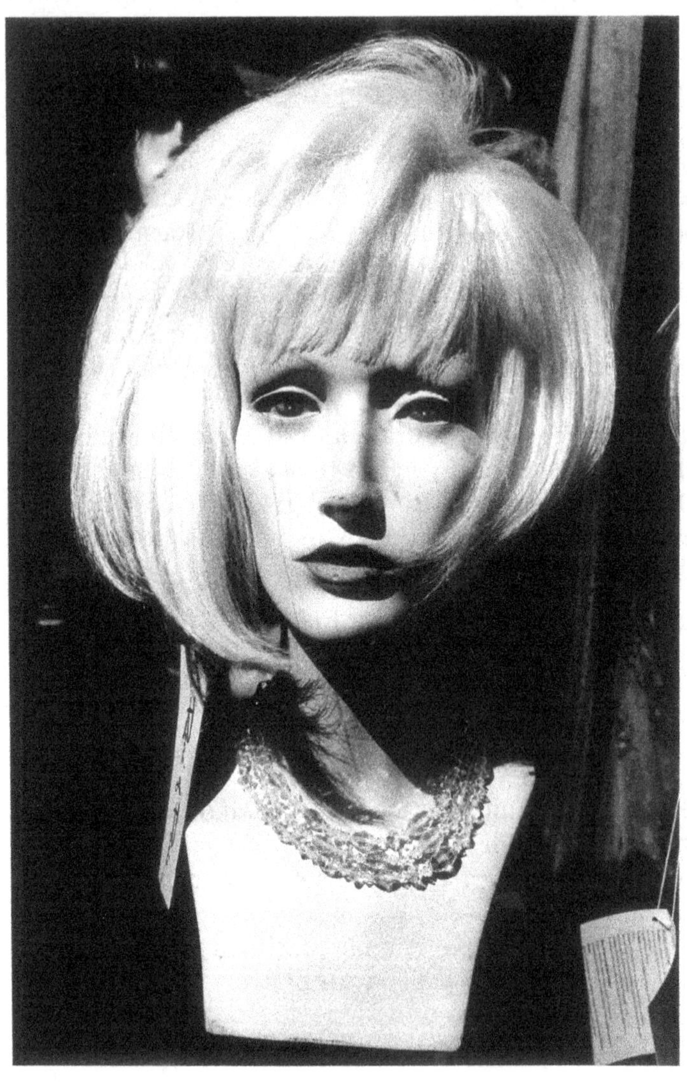

Photo: Yoshi Yubai

[laughs] Except that now it's four-thirty p.m. Maybe they'd work until six, and then I'd go down there or back up to the Chelsea, or whatever. And *I* would go at ten o'clock to my apartment down on 9th Street and Avenue B and work on the sound poems or whatever I was working on.

The nights would be filled with parties and—

That was my aim: just having dinner in Chinatown. There was one Chinese restaurant where William liked to eat *every night.*

How come? Was there a really good bar?

No, he liked the food. There was no bar. It was one of those places where the entire meal—having everything—was three dollars or even (this was 1965) $2.75, you know—

Oh, I love places like that... Or two dollars!

Or a dollar-fifty. Or a dollar, actually!

I think you could eat for a dollar then.

Uh-huh... $2.75 was having an enormous banquet! But it was one of those where you had to walk downstairs; there was no bar. Brion would often not want to do that because he'd had enough of William all day, and he'd come back to the Chelsea. Or, Panna Grady would give one of her great, fantastic parties.

Was there ever any "open sex" at any of these affairs?

No.

Really? It was all well-behaved; nothing wild?

William was 52 and Brion was 50, I think… twenty-one years have passed, so William is 72 now, and this was… whatever. [laughs]

Do you remember any wild parties during the Warhol sixties?

There were never orgies, you know. Because this is

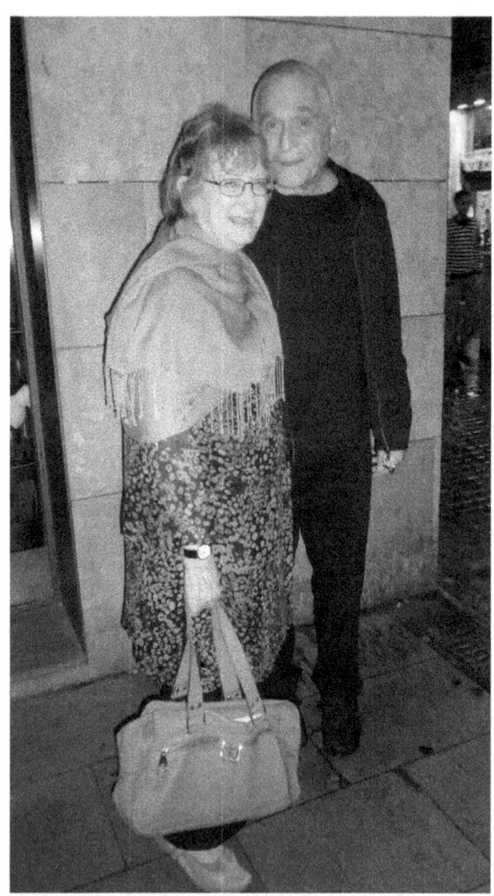

John Giorno with Claire Walsh, J.G. Ballard's late girlfriend, in Barcelona

coming *right* out of the fifties! It was before anyone did *that*. For instance, in '67 or something when I did that pornographic poem, that was incredibly courageous. A found poem with that kind of obscenity… it was sort of like *taking the bull by the horns*. It was just a matter of *two years* before the idea of "open sexuality" happened. But between those two or three years was an enormous change in the culture.

Then it hit the movies in 1973 with *Deep Throat*. Of course, now we're trying to get back to the fifties with Ed Meese here—

And the Supreme Court now… I don't really care, because when something goes completely in the opposite direction, it becomes hotter for the other side. Makes what one's doing sexually sort of intenser.

Well, yeah, but you don't want to go to jail, either. Like, Jello Biafra is in a hell of a lot of trouble for putting that HR Giger poster in his album—that sex painting.

Do you have that here, by any chance? I'd like to see it. I got the album in New York but it didn't have the poster in it!

I just had a long talk to Biafra today; I'll try to get one from him—I'm sure there aren't *any* at his house! Defending yourself against obscenity charges is so expensive, and if you "win" nobody pays you back for all those legal fees. Plus, he can't even write songs now—it's very hard to do that with all this hanging over him.

Back to Warhol: you must have learned things from him? Like, he has this persona of being "real shy"—maybe that's a good defense. Makes it hard to

talk to him.

I see Andy really seldom, but I've seen him a couple of times in the last years, and he comes off exactly the same. *Because* I don't see him very often, he'll instantly start talking about "one January when he started a new painting and went out to an auction and"—suddenly he launches us into remembrances of something that happened long ago. Andy's got this great memory; he remembers *everything,* like some little thing that happened in '63.

I really liked his *Philosophy From A to B*—those short little observances. He obviously has an interior life—just writing those things down takes time by yourself...

Back to Brion: talk about some of the LSD trips you took together—that's such a wild thing! There wasn't yet a *theory*—it wasn't totally spelled out as to what you might do—

They were *completely sexual trips,* you know! Outside of the sexual, would be these incredible hallucinations, because this was really early, *pure* acid. These experiences were something which conditioned *my whole life,* because Brion *talked* all the time, and would endlessly be *telling you things*... which laid a *foundation* for everything I have thought since, or at least worked with since.

He must have been one of several people who opened your eyes to this alternative culture—

Actually, the thing was: I was this *kid,* you know—stupid like all kids are stupid, particularly since there was nothing *there* that was coming out of the fifties. So taking these completely hallucinogenic trips opened up the possibility of *other realms,* you know.

My father died in January. I was out on a tour of

England for two weeks, and when I got back the phone rang the next day—my father had died that day. I wrote this to Brion, and he wrote back a very moving letter saying that somebody who wasn't an enemy but wasn't a friend—he was an *unfriend*, who he had known for all these years—had gotten Alzheimer's disease and gone across the street to the building, gone up to the top and jumped off. And Brion had seen it—he didn't see him fall, but one second later saw this person at the bottom. And he kept saying, "I've lost my chance to kill myself, because I don't have the energy anymore—or the *power* anymore—to do that."

Brion, as you know, was endlessly talking about committing suicide. The next sentence was something about (I can't remember the words) "those trips that we took together" meaning those ones in '65. We *know* there are other realms that one goes to when one dies, which was another reason that he wasn't sure about killing himself: whether he *could*, or what would happen if he *did*. It was very moving. I was so glad at the end that he didn't kill himself.

Hmm... He must have "turned you on" to all this other kind of music that he knows so much about.

During the trips, he would have the tapes from Joujouka which we'd play endlessly—

On acid.

Yeah. He'd brought lots of music, a dozen tapes with him.

He'd tell you stories, I guess—

Great tales! Brion was a great story-teller. The nature of the stories had sort of a *teaching*, so they were these endless *teachings* we got. And I probably was the person there by chance, by circumstance—it could have been anyone else because Brion was essentially *talking to himself*—spouting all this wisdom, so to speak.

Then I went to Morocco in February of '66 and lived with Brion until I got a house where I worked every day in the Casbah. During that six months we were endlessly on trips down south to the Joujouka pipes of Pan (or whatever it was called) during our seven-day period with the Joujouka. And then lots of other trips down to Marrakesh and the Sahara and back.

For the six months, every two weeks by chance somebody was coming through Tangiers going somewhere. This guy in Morocco who lived in Fez was going home, so Brion and I would get in the car and go to Fez and go to those music things that were happening. I had brought along a whole bunch of LSD from New York.

Did you actually take LSD in those alien settings? I guess you didn't feel they were "alien," though?

That didn't enter into my mind—it was beyond any thought like that! We had this one memorable trip in Fez, where we went down with this guy because his family lived there and he had an apartment with a guest room, so we stayed. One day we took some acid and went up to the tombs—you know how Fez is sort of this circular thing that goes down, and there are cliffs all around it? On top of the cliffs are these tombs, and we arrived there near sunset.

We went up there, and that's when the acid *hit!* It was sort of amazing because it was a long, complicated road, and you had to go out of Fez and around to the other side of the cliffs. Now they've built a hotel up there and it's become this tourist hole. But there was no way there, and you'd hear these dogs barking in these houses back and down the hill of the mountain, and on the other side. You couldn't walk that way because they were half-jackal and half-dog—they protect the little farms. So we had to climb down the face of the cliff in the blackness, which was *magnificent*, with Fez down there.

We get down there to one of the main gates of Fez and go in. Fez goes down in a circle. It winds like a spiral down to the bottom, Fez being what they call "the religious capital of Morocco." As you go down, you go down through the centuries because the city was built from this small stream down at the bottom. It took us four or five hours to wind down in a circle to the ancient Fez which was probably five thousand years old or something, the two of us endlessly talking about one thing or another.

The next day we got back to the Savannah. So with acid, you wake up after a few hours... We went to bed really late and woke up really early and went back up with nothing to do because we were in the Savannah in Fez, so we took a taxi back up to the tombs. That night, apparently, somebody had broken into one of the tombs and dug it up and stolen whatever was there except these bones (presumably from one of the kings) which I scooped up in this handkerchief I had. I still have them, believe it or not, in New York. They were really ancient, these arm bones and leg bones—they were so old that they were completely brittle. They looked brittle, they were almost fossilized.

Did you meet all those other storytellers? Hamri, you know—Mohamed Hamri.

Hamri and Choukri and everyone was there.

They were all there! Wait—what did they speak? What language? They only speak French at the most, right?

They all spoke English.

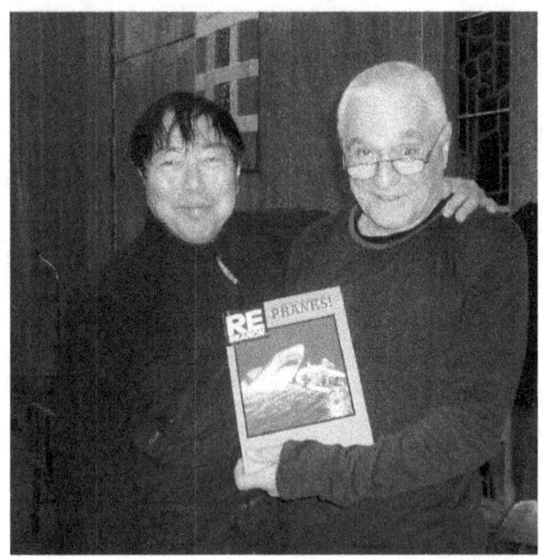

V. Vale and John Giorno, in San Francisco

And Mrabet too?

A little bit, because Paul lived upstairs from Brion and during that six months he wasn't on such good terms with him, so…

With Brion?

No, Paul and Mrabet. I only met him twice, I think.

Tangiers was really awful in those years. Morocco was great, every place we went, you couldn't believe; but Tangiers was sort of a dead city, nothing was happening there the way that legend leads one to believe. I said that to Paul once. "It's totally horrible here! Why do you guys live here?" Paul said, "John, for us it's as if somebody rang a great gong twenty-five years ago, and we still hear the timbre of the sound!" My thought was (I don't think I ever *said* it), "Great… if you were here twenty-five years ago! *I* don't hear *nothing!*"

Tangiers I guess is worse now… Again, it was

great for a short time—maybe ten years. At the end of WWII Tangiers was the international zone; it was totally "hot" because everyone had come from Europe to escape *whatever* and it was a "free zone." That went through the forties—even in the fifties it still had that incredible energy. But by '66 it was *gone*.

William writes about that feeling in *Naked Lunch*. How did you support yourself then? Did you have a little job or something?

It was really cheap. For a hundred and fifty dollars a month, you could live like you had fifteen hundred dollars in New York. The rent was thirty-five dollars, Con Ed [utilities] was twelve, telephone was twelve, and dope was ten or twelve dollars, food was... so for a hundred and fifty dollars a month one could live there very easily.

It's really great that you got to be with Brion there. Then what happened? You just got tired of being there? You got tired of all the music and exploring?

Yeah. The whole thing just *ended* for me—six months is a long time! All these things were happening in New York, which I sort of wanted to get back to.

So how did Brion get along with Paul Bowles?

Really well. He didn't get along too well with Jane [Bowles], but Paul and he were great friends.

Was Bowles really helpful to everybody? Wasn't he like the resident "host" of the place, because he'd been there so long?

He and Brion were sort of the same. They lived very quiet

lives. Did you ever see where they lived? It was opposite the Consulate; a very modern building built by the Italians probably in the 1940s. It was a modern Italian apartment. The rooms were really small; the biggest room was just the size of this area here. Jane had one extra room. Paul used to come down every day and stop in, he was on the floor above and he'd take one of those little European elevators that go up so he didn't have to walk down, while he was getting his mail and *whatnot.* He still lives, to this day, in that apartment.

I'd like to go there before it's too late. Someone I knew went to Morocco and landed in jail, and Paul Bowles got him out. It was the poet Philip Lamantia; I think that was in the fifties. He was kind of grateful to Paul Bowles—I guess Bowles had some sort of "connections," otherwise Philip could have been there forever. I think it was something to do with hash, which is *kind of* legal but not legal, right?

Even though in those years… in the sixties, nobody smoked hash. Moroccans really sort of hate hash, including everyone like Brion, at the time.

That's right—it's not hash, is it?

It's kief.

Kief! That's right.

Sometimes some of the hash settles at the bottom of the bag so it's as strong as keif. It's like what Ezra Pound says, "It's always at the bottom of the bag." Well, they used to say, "Nobody ever smoked hash other than crazy American girls!" Hash makes you crazy; keif doesn't. All Moroccans think that.

What's the difference between keif and hash?

Keif is really grass but they put the pollen in with the leaves or something—some kind of blend. Hash is just the *pollen* made into…

Oh, so it's probably too strong! Concentrated.

Any Moroccan thinks that hash makes you crazy, even though they probably smoke it on occasion. But not so much.

Every day when you woke up with Brion, whenever time every morning when you woke up in Tangier (at ten o'clock or ten-thirty or whatever) the first thing was the tea, you know? And while you're having your tea you have the Sebsi—the long pipe… you have two or three hits of the pipe, which would take care of the next hour of fiddling around—taking a shower, or whatever. And then the day began.

I realized that we all smoked, but that was probably the root of Brion's emphysema. Besides cigarettes (which we all smoked) we were having those *really* [inhales sharply] strong Sebsis every morning, which Brion had every day of his life. When I saw Brion ten days before he died and I started smoking, he looked at me in this outrageous way and said, "*What are you doing?* Look at me! Do you want this to happen to *you?*" But he said it in a way that wasn't like one of those people saying, "What are you smoking for? Do you want to get lung cancer?" It was some other motive: "Do you want this to happen?" Which was the first time I'd ever heard Brion say such a thing.

Yeah, I had to run out and get Brion cigarettes last time I was there.

When I was there, he'd take a puff or two, or three or four. It didn't matter—it was at *the end,* so who cared?

You said that after he got the medical verdict that he was carcinogenic, or what do you call it?

He was "positive."

Positive—then he was sort of *focused and calm.*

Well, that's what Fafa said. I asked Brion, "What's happening today?" and he said, "The doctors just left… It was positive." That was all he said…

The very second that you're dying you might have one little thought (and Brion had many of them) of anger, you know? You may have been peaceful *for years* before you die, but it just takes one moment of malicious thought or anger… and that's what you've got.

I frequently think about William Burroughs's statement, "Death often presents the face of surprised recognition." Anyway… would you say that it's *not easy* to get close to William?

William is very difficult to get close to. I didn't get that close to him in those early years, because I was *Brion's* friend! It wasn't until when William came back in for the Nova Convention that we sort of really formed a friendship. Terry Southern had a house in New York and was out of town, so William would stay there. I'd go over for dinner; it was just for a few months. Then we went back to London, and whenever I was in town I'd stop to visit him. And he'd come back—it was a little "back and forth."

Did he ever talk to you about "creative problems"—like, "John, I just can't seem to end this book right!" [laughs] Stuff like that?

All the time—to this day! You know, *The Western Lands*

is finished, and it's all on the computer and it's all printed out and everything. The book has been stymied for almost a year—or at least nine months. Maybe half of the connections between the various sections hadn't yet been written! We went to Germany, and it still hadn't been finished, and then they were going to take it to Boulder...

William is just like everyone else: he talks about getting writer's block where you feel like you could never, ever write again, not another word! I think he has it all the time. Although when he breaks it, he goes through endless months (or years) of not having writer's block. He's just endlessly creative. Because William writes every day. When he gets into something, he sits in front of that typewriter, writing down every word.

Has he learned how to use a word processor?

No, it gets transferred onto a word processor. So then when he corrects it and rewrites it, it's easy to get another finished page.

That's how he's working now?! So John, did William get you interested in guns?

Um... No. [laughs]

Or are you more of an observer in that department?

A little bit more of an *observant*. Among other reasons: I come from New York, where it's not in the culture there. There's no place to *do it,* you know?

Yeah, you can't go shooting anywhere—

And so—if you don't get into it early, I think, it's not something you can *do*. And William did. So down at the Bunker, William would endlessly get that little—you know that little gun?

Pellet pistol?

Pellet pistol! I mean, that's just some sort of extension of some habit. Whereas if you don't have the habit, it's great to do whenever you do it, but it's not something you'd do *yourself.*

Right. Yeah, I would have liked to have grown up fishing, for example. I tried fishing once, and it was just so boring.

I know!

I couldn't do it.

William has a little rowboat down in Lawrence, which actually… a month ago I spoke to him and he said, "Why the hell do I have that boat?" Fishing? Can you imagine fishing on a little lake in Kansas? God, I'd rather die! And I've seen him, on the *rare* occasion when we've been out in the country, and he actually *likes* to have this line in the water… I suppose with fishing there is very little expectation, but… my line's not in the water!

I know… all that wisdom you're supposed to acquire when fishing: "Fishing is like life." Have you ever gone with William to a bookstore? What does he look for?

The only reason he goes into bookstores is to buy one of those pocketbooks—those airport-bookstore pocketbooks… spy stuff.
Oh, he reads lots of those?

Mm-hmm. When on tour he's always going into those

stores in the airports, trying to find a book. It's almost like he's—

Dowsing?

Dowsing. And he's read so many of those books—it's the only thing he reads!

Right! How does he find the time to write and read and do all this?

Well, it's just those times when you have nothing to do, and you sit down and watch the news—watch TV. You keep changing the channels, or call somebody on the telephone. William *hates* the telephone, so he never calls anyone other than somebody he *has* to call, or *wants* to...

Other than Brion. He used to call Brion.

Of course he calls Brion. But those were *monumental* things, you know. Every two months or so he would have a few vodkas and this would be the dowser day to call Brion. [laughs] When he calls he doesn't talk that long—he's not like the way you and I do it.

He *never* watches television, other than maybe *National Geographic*, nature shows. What he does is sit in a chair with one of those wretched pocketbooks that he reads on the airplane, that he reads in the hotel room, and... that's his reading habits.

That's very interesting: the idea of breaking the telephone habit. I hadn't thought of trying that.

He never had a telephone habit! Did you ever have an old great-aunt?! William actually talks like an old great-aunt of mine: he holds the telephone almost two or three inches from his ear, three or four inches from his mouth, and it's like a nineteenth-century going into twentieth-century—the way older people talk. He still does it to this day! That's why he feels uncomfortable with the telephone. That's how he looks when he does it!

That's fantastic; I love it—

—rather than doing what you and I do, which is to fall on your bed, put your head back, and have the telephone pressed to your ear—

Well, little things like that could mean freeing up a lot of time!

But it also means a lack of being able to… William is like somebody's great-grandfather who grew up in another time, because living in Morocco and places like in Paris, 9 Rue Gît-le-Cœur, there's no telephone in the room—he never got those habits because it just wasn't there! It was only in the 1960s that the telephone was there all the time for you to use if you wanted to.

That's kind of amazing. You've never been in a situation with William where he had to defend himself, have you?

[shakes his head]

Good! I'm glad to hear that.

I don't think *he's* ever been in that situation, either.

That's good!

Well… once he was going to a supermarket, and he had turned on the corner of Bowery onto Springsteen—

Oh, in New York.

Yes. And this kid had a coat jacket on, and he put his hand in the side pocket and said, "Give me your money" (or whatever). William, being the old William, *knew* there wasn't a gun there, and raised his hand and pushed his finger inside the pocket. [laughs] And the kid just looked like an idiot!

That's fantastic!

That's his *one* scrape with danger! [laughs] Otherwise, he's totally protected. Whatever kind of magic or "protection" he surrounds himself with, danger (the *real* kind of danger) never really enters to threaten him.

Yeah, all right, and may it continue. That's great! But he got me that little Cobra [a telescoping baton for self-defense].

Well, that's not saying that *every* second he leaves the Bunker (or even when we're coming to visit him in Lawrence, Kansas), that he doesn't go out without that Cobra thing… and the stun gun, I guess.

Oh, does he have a stun gun now?

He was the first! Literally, long before the police department had it—he read in one of those magazines that you guys get him, and he sent away his $69 or whatever and got it—

No kidding!

And he showed it off—and it was before you even *heard* the word "stun gun"!

Right. Good ol' William. [Both Vale and Giorno laugh] That's fantastic! Yeah, I'm anxious to hear any little thing I can learn from Burroughs.

Even when he was a junky, he could always protect himself?

Well, he's got this sort of *invisible* quality—today I'm sure it's the same as it was back then. I always think it's the way he carries all of these armaments: between the stun gun and the Cobra, and the "poker"—some kind of knife that can poke you, or just a piece of wood that he carries around to stick somebody right in between the ribcage. [laughs]

"Prepare your lawyers immediately!"

But they become metaphoric, symbolic armaments… like Tibetan deities, where they have six or eight arms, and each holds a certain *something* which represents a kind of protection or power. I always think of *William* as a kind of deity having all these symbolic armaments which *indeed* may be symbolic, but...

They work!

Well, they manifest power in a little thing that looks like nothing, but...

It's amazing how strong he is, too. He's so thin, but very strong. Like, all wiry. Instead of becoming fat and old, just shrink down to muscle and bone and nerve!

Well, in his own words: "I have a great fear of being fat."
V: Oh, he said that?

Many times! He's always eaten very little… he doesn't eat

that much.

I know!

It's actually because he has this *fear* of becoming fat! Which is probably something lots of WASP people have. And the reason being he has that genetically thin WASP thing—like those little WASP ladies, you know... what comes to mind is when he was inducted into the American Academy of Arts and Letters—or whenever there is an important meeting or an important party... he makes sure we have our Cobras before we leave... [laughs]

That's great—he probably knows something I don't.

It's fine! I always think he's *empowered* these things—even though they are these dumb little things that you have on your belt, they are *empowered* in some incredible way.

Maybe if you have something like that on you, you radiate a different psychic defense? Maybe a lot of criminals are like animals who can just *sense* fear—

But that's *his* armor. We all do it in our own way, and that's his particular way of manifesting power or protection.

Whenever I'm around him, I like to always be looking around. You think that he's kind of old and fragile. [both Vale and Giorno laugh] "That's right, I'm tougher than you are!"

Let's pick up the thread with Brion. You left Morocco in 1966, and then what?

Then I saw Brion only when I went to Paris for my very first tours.

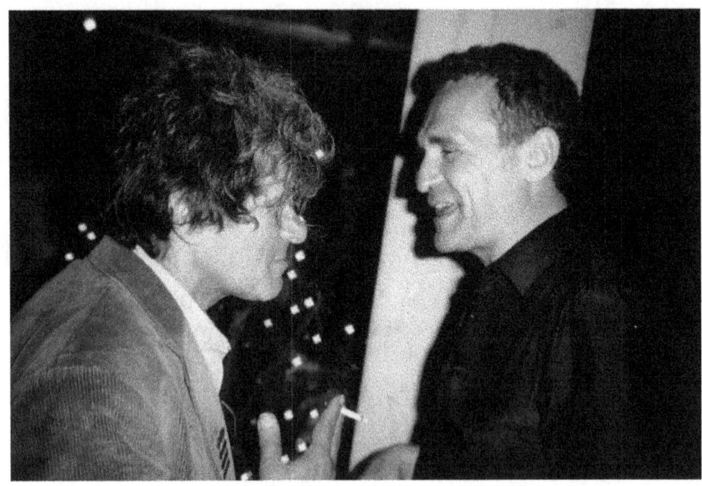

Gregory Corso and John Giorno, San Francisco

Oh! And those began when?

From the late sixties on—1970 and 1972; whenever there would be some festival. And I always made the point—even though I wasn't going there—to stop in Paris and visit Brion. One time I was coming back from India on Pan Am and had a two-hour layover. I called Brion at 5 in the morning [laughs] and said, "I'm here, can I come over?"

Even though it was weirdly quick, we probably smoked some joints and I got back to the airport. This is kind of personal, but sometimes I didn't *want* to see him because of how much anger he had toward me. But the times when I really adored seeing him, I would spend as much time as I could with him—three or four days.

Brion always triggers these things that draw you to him, and whenever *that* happens… I might go to Paris once or twice a year, almost every year. I always want to see Brion. And the last time, I can't believe I was there when he died.

Yeah... Did he ever take any other photos of you like the ones you gave me? I didn't even know he was a photographer—

Him taking that picture—I'm sure it wasn't even his camera... somebody must have had it. It was the day he was leaving, and there was a camera in the room—because Brion wasn't even a photographer.

When you called William today, he told you about the Dylan thing—

Only that Dylan has this concert Thursday night—

Yeah, it was on the news!

Burroughs is going to meet me at the Kansas City Airport, and we'll stay in Kansas City for the concert. Dylan and William got along, so...

Oh!

Brion's dying was really important to William—more important than Billy [Burroughs, Jr.] dying, you know?

Yeah, of course. Definitely affected *me*.

And this will probably be the last time we'll talk about Brion. William has a thing: when somebody dies, he stops talking about 'em. When Billy died during the trip: a few tears, and, uh—he's never mentioned Billy's name again!

That's great—I love that.

So this time, after this thing, Brion will be like Billy! When his name comes up, or if anyone says something, it's finished—like, never to be spoken again...

That's like some tribe I was reading about recently: when someone dies, they never speak the name of the dead person again. Maybe that makes sense. So, can you tell me anything more about Brion's last days?

Well, Brion got really stoned from a bunch of great grass.

When Brion smokes, it certainly doesn't affect his powers of verbalization—

It did at one point, actually! Fafa told me that Brion got a bit incoherent, and the nurse was saying, "If he loses his mind, that's *really* bad." Fafa said, "He didn't!" Other than being a little incoherent, he came right back… but apparently he couldn't talk very well *at the end.* Or, if you couldn't hear what he said, you'd irritate Brion because he'd have to say it again… and he had so little energy.

Right.

But there was one *totally* coherent moment… One moment when that joint really hit, Brion did one of those things that used to be so great—suddenly he was talking about Eleanor of Aquitaine, and then it was William the Conqueror, then it was the Crusades, then some Byzantine King, and then it was back to Eleanor of Aquitaine… and I was sitting there thinking, "I'm completely missing something! He's telling me something important, but I have *no idea* what he's talking about!" And then I realized that actually, he was talking about *love!* He was talking about how Eleanor of Aquitaine had introduced love for the first time in… It was all narrative about great Kings and Princes.

That's one thing: if I die, I want to be lucid to the end.

David Wells was there—this was just a little moment, you know? I understood as far as Eleanor of Aquitaine, and suddenly there was William the Conqueror... and suddenly there was the Duke of...

In Paris I stayed with my friend Bruno who lives a block and a half from Brion. He's always lived there, and it was so close to Brion—it was just effortless. *Literally*, a block and a half.

Brion's apartment is gone by the end of the month. Presumably, the paintings are out by last Friday, and David Wells is the little guy who's left with all the household things to move out.

Brion was telling us about how the landlord wanted him out of there because he could get so much more rent.

I'm sure, because he wasn't paying that much.

Hey, they have rent control in New York at your place, right?

Yeah. Better than rent control—we're rent stabilized, which is the same, but the building has to be "sealed." All the violations have to be gone before they can raise the rent. So when William left... The Bunker is $355 a month—the *same* as it was when William left! They can't raise the rent—remember, you have to get rid of every violation before they allow you to raise the rent by seven percent! [laughs] For three days I'm visiting William, and then I'm coming back to New York on Sunday.

Yeah, Allen Ginsberg is going to be there.

He arrived yesterday, I think?

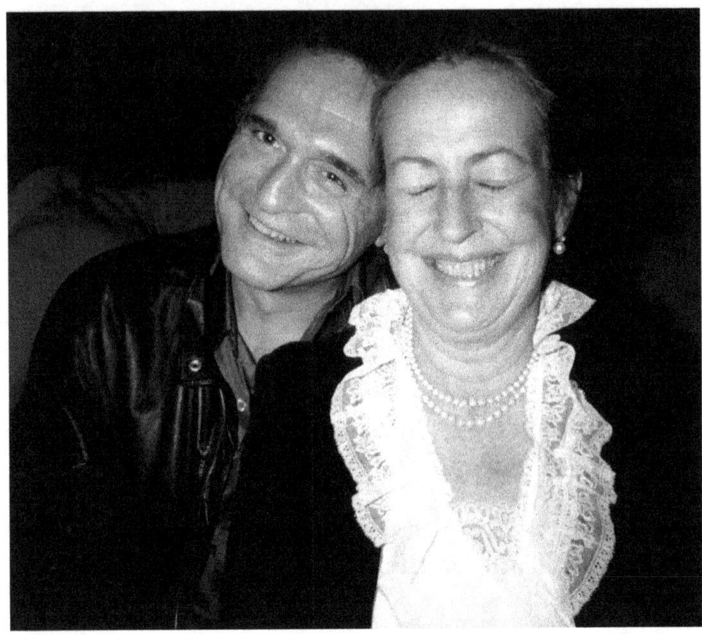

John Giorno with Felicity Mason

—and I think they were moving. Or did they move?

Yeah, it was in Lawrence. It's a long story. When we got back from Germany, apparently they just got back in Kansas and got an eviction notice… and we had thirty days to get everything out. So we moved everything out, and in that thirty days he decided to buy the third house. [laughs] So they're in the process of closing in on a third house where they will store the archive. They're about to close title on the third house, but none of it is quite there—you have to refinance the whole thing. It's three things rather than two now.

Hey, do you know how Felicity Mason met Brion? They must go back twenty or thirty years—

They go back *forty* years or something—

Wow! I'll have to talk to Felicity.

Actually, she mentioned it once, but it's not coming back to me how they met—they had friends in common, or whatever it was. And they were born a year apart in Greenwich, England—or maybe their birthday is roughly within a month of each other.

Hey John, you'll never bring back your out-of-print records?

It costs so much money, and they don't sell that well.

I know what you mean—yeah, I know *all* about it. Maybe you can do cassette reissues, because you can strike those off when you get orders. You can buy a cheap cassette duplicator—

Ah, give me a break—I've got enough problems!

[Giorno and Vale laugh]

next page: W.S. Burroughs at Chabot Range

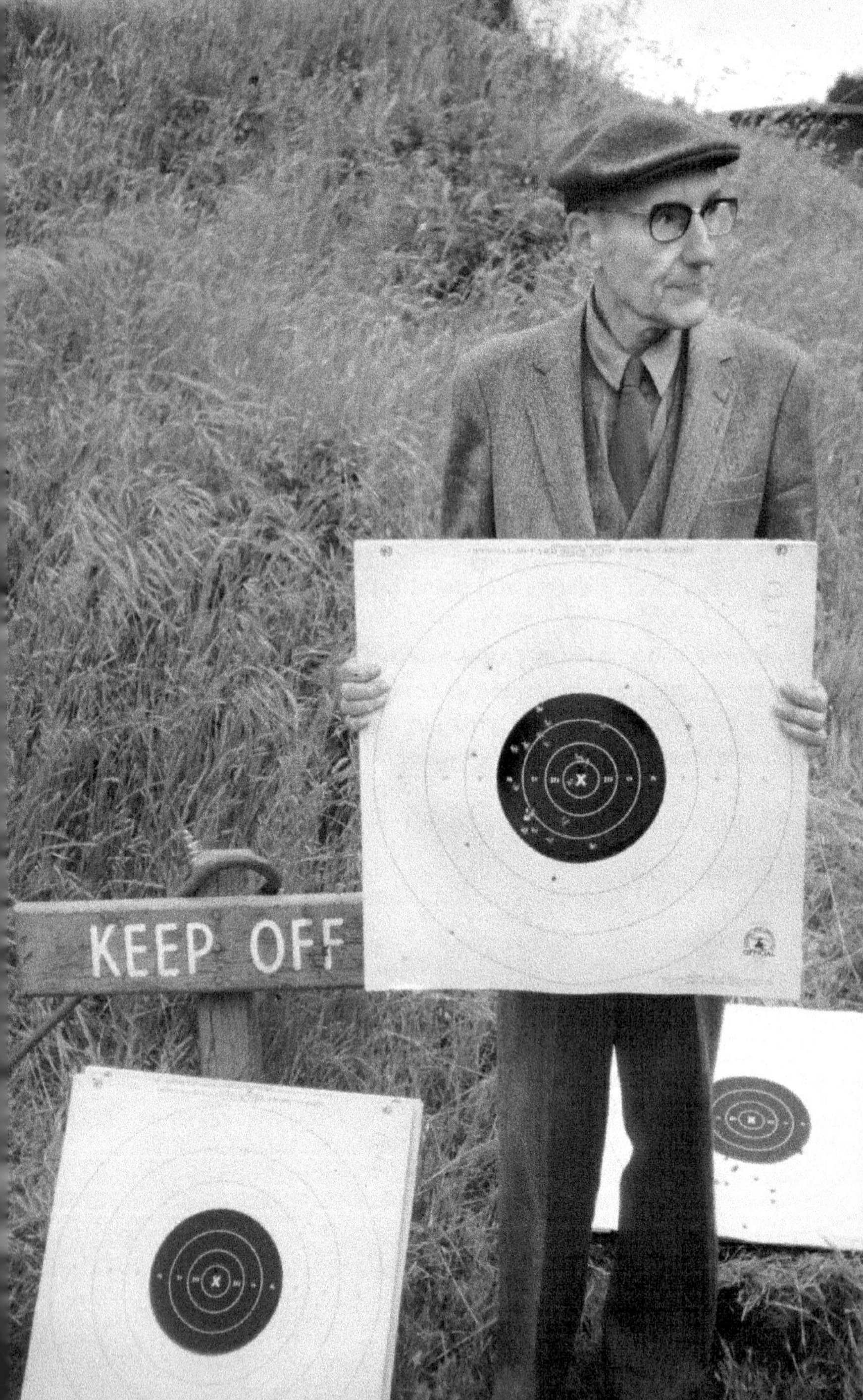
KEEP OFF

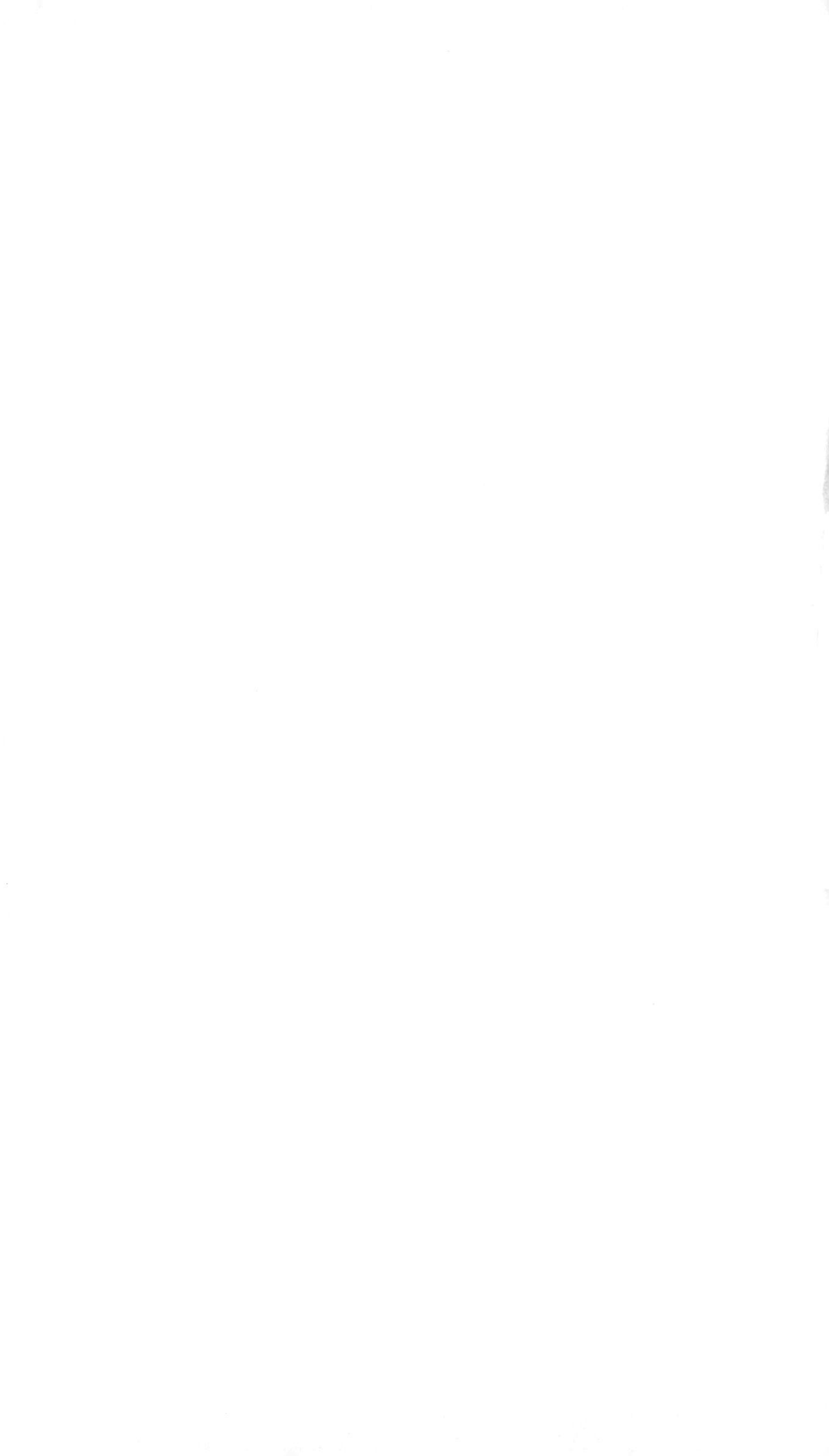

www.ingramcontent.com/pod-product-compliance
Lightning Source LLC
Jackson TN
JSHW080445240725
88124JS00002B/2